Fundamentals
for the Instruction
Coordinator

ALA FUNDAMENTALS SERIES

FUNDAMENTALS FOR THE ACADEMIC LIAISON
by Richard Moniz, Jo Henry, and Joe Eshleman

FUNDAMENTALS FOR THE INSTRUCTION COORDINATOR
by Caitlin A. Bagley

FUNDAMENTALS OF CHILDREN'S SERVICES, 2ND ED.
by Michael Sullivan

FUNDAMENTALS OF ELECTRONIC RESOURCES MANAGEMENT
by Alana Verminski and Kelly Marie Blanchat

FUNDAMENTALS OF LIBRARY INSTRUCTION
by Monty L. McAdoo

FUNDAMENTALS OF LIBRARY SUPERVISION, 3RD ED.
by Beth McNeil

FUNDAMENTALS OF MANAGING REFERENCE COLLECTIONS
by Carol A. Singer

FUNDAMENTALS OF PLANNING AND ASSESSMENT FOR LIBRARIES
by Rachel A. Fleming-May and Regina Mays

FUNDAMENTALS OF REFERENCE
by Carolyn M. Mulac

FUNDAMENTALS OF TECHNICAL SERVICES
by John Sandstrom and Liz Miller

FUNDAMENTALS OF TECHNICAL SERVICES MANAGEMENT
by Sheila S. Intner, with Peggy Johnson

SMALL PUBLIC LIBRARY MANAGEMENT
by Jane Pearlmutter and Paul Nelson

ALA FUNDAMENTALS SERIES

Fundamentals for the Instruction Coordinator

Caitlin A. Bagley

ALA Neal-Schuman

Chicago 2022

CAITLIN A. BAGLEY is an associate professor and instruction librarian at Gonzaga University in Spokane. Her research has focused on shifting library technologies and most recently on using infographics in instruction. She has authored several articles on cloud computing and infographics. She is a 2013 ACRL Immersion Teaching with Technology graduate. Bagley earned her master's degree in library science at Indiana University.

© 2022 by Caitlin A. Bagley

Extensive effort has gone into ensuring the reliability of the information in this book; however, the publisher makes no warranty, express or implied, with respect to the material contained herein.

ISBN: 978-0-8389-1637-7 (paper)

Library of Congress Cataloging-in-Publication Data on file

Book design in the Melior and Din typefaces. Cover image © Adobe Stock, Inc.

♾ This paper meets the requirements of ANSI/NISO Z39.48-1992 (Permanence of Paper).

Printed in the United States of America
26 25 24 23 22   5 4 3 2 1

ALA Neal-Schuman purchases fund advocacy, awareness, and accreditation programs for library professionals worldwide.

Contents

Preface

Like so much of the work in academic libraries, instruction is a team effort. Our collective skills include teaching, curricular expertise, diplomacy, instruction design, and project management. Like any team, we cover for each other. While institutions vary in how they assign duties, the common goal is the organizational ability to develop information literacy skills of students and supporting faculty and their curricula. Job titles vary widely across institutions, including the title *instruction coordinator*. No matter the job title, somebody must lead the effort and see that the finer details of the instructional offering—whether it is accommodating a class in a lab, teaching a one-shot, or leading a library orientation—are taken care of. For purposes of this book, that person is the instructional coordinator.

The goal of this book is to serve as a general introduction to librarians new to the job of instruction coordinator or those assuming some of those duties along with their instruction specialty. In libraries where these duties are parceled out to more than one person, readers can use this book as a reference, zeroing in on their critical duties. Collaboration will always be a big part of the instruction coordinator's job. From managing to faculty outreach, the instruction coordinator will work with many different personalities and roles across the university. Communication and working with people are common themes throughout the book.

I have been an instructional coordinator since 2016. My first day as instructional coordinator I was filling in for a colleague on sabbatical. I was familiar with the workings of our department, but as calls came in to schedule classes, I soon felt overwhelmed with the details of the job. Success as a coordinator requires excellent organizational skills and the ability to juggle multiple projects. I hope this book will help you establish the systems that work for you.

Though I work at a small, private university, I have previous experience at a large state university. I know first-hand that instruction is handled differently among libraries. For that reason, I interviewed fourteen librarians from a range of institutions to get background for this book.

I wrote this book before the pandemic. Libraries and higher ed in general were compelled to change the way we work in an incredibly short period of time. Online instruction already was part of our toolbox and became the predominant form in no time. The acceleration of that trend is likely to continue. I was surprised in reviewing the book how many of our online instructional technologies were in place prior to the pandemic. Librarians are skilled at finding ways to embrace change, but the pandemic made clear Instruction coordinators must stay up on technology and be ready to collaborate with technology teams to offers solutions and meet expectations.

Instruction coordinators need to be flexible. If you master the fundamentals, you will be in good shape to thrive in this always evolving role.

1

The Landscape of Instruction Coordination

Introduction

Hello. Are you an instruction coordinator? If so, can you verbalize your instruction philosophy? Is it written down for everyone in your department to see? Can it be processed and seen within the work of the librarians who carry out information literacy courses? If, as I once was, you are still sitting there wondering what an instruction philosophy is and why anyone in your department would want to see it, this book is for you. This book looks at the practical day-to-day functions of being an instruction coordinator as well as perspectives on how to interpret the larger events of the information literacy landscape as they happen, such as the more pedagogical twists of the framework and what it means to be a teacher librarian.

As I thought about the fundamental practices of an instruction coordinator, I quickly realized there would be differences among types of institutions. Certainly, I knew from my own experiences that a small private library runs far differently than a large state university. I started by surveying instruction librarians. Then, to learn more about practices and common approaches, I interviewed fourteen coordinators from a range of settings and with varied experiences. You can find these survey questions in the appendix. In chapter 8, "Best Practices," I share examples and summaries of their responses to demonstrate what works and what does not.

On my first day as an instruction coordinator, I was filling in for a colleague on sabbatical. In terms of preparation, I had more time to get ready for the job than most people usually do. I had access to a network of resources, I was familiar with the university system, and I thought I understood the general principle of what was about to happen, but then reality hit me: people began requesting classes, and all my preconceptions flew out the window. The first few requests were fine—I put those on the calendar and assigned them with ease—but then the little details began to pile up. Faculty began asking me several questions: Do the computers in the lab have this specific program (of course, one I had never used before)? Can this or that department have a training session in the labs? Oh, and would it be an issue if it was catered? And by the way, did you know the lab needs to be redesigned, and you have to approve the plans? By the end of my first semester in the role, all I could think was: *There needs to be a manual for this stuff.* Even the best prepared of us will falter and search for answers; no manual can predict every scenario. But the goal of this book is to help instruction coordinators address common situations and give them the tools to prepare for the unpredictable ones.

The formal title of an instruction coordinator can differ depending on your institution. You might be called an instruction coordinator, or you might have friends who do the same job as you, but they are referred to as information literacy coordinators or teaching and learning program librarians, you might even have other job duties beyond information literacy. But no matter the title, you all handle the finer details of how instruction is performed at your library. Information literacy has been part of the library for a long time, but like instruction coordination, it has worn many different hats and titles. From the humble title "research," to "library instruction," and everything in between, instruction coordinators (the position term predominately used in this book) have come to act as the leads who arrange the finer details of instruction within and even sometimes outside of the library. This can include one-shot instruction sessions, orientations, tours, and even beginning-of-the-year library-wide events. Because of this breadth, as an instruction coordinator, it is essential for you to bring coherence to a group of librarians who must perform all types of instruction. You set the tone for how your department is perceived not only within the library but on the whole campus, for your work will reach far and wide across the institution. As I looked for instruction coordinators to talk to for this book, one of the most common things I heard was "It's not part of my title, but I do that job." It is frustrating to hear people undervalue themselves when they do such amazing and important work as coordinators. Discussing our frustrations and problems with the role can help us fix these things and make us more aware of why the role matters both to us and to the larger library field.

Lest you be intimidated, know that being an instruction coordinator can also be enormously fun. At its best, the role allows you the potential to talk to people all across campus who have bright ideas, high hopes, enthusiasm, and wit about education. You will also work in concert with professors and departmental heads, which will allow you to learn more than you ever thought possible about specific instructional needs by department. Your team will look to you as a leader to help guide them through difficult instruction scenarios, perhaps a professor who is requesting more than is possible or a student who is having difficulty grasping concepts, or in offering guidance on how to teach specific lessons. Frequently, coordinators work with partners across campus who do not appear to be naturally aligned; other partners, such as athletics, marketing, and the first-year experience, might all align naturally with your work. Part of the goal of this book is to point out how you can network successfully with campus partners so that each can form a mutually beneficial relationship with the library.

Instruction has come a long way in the world of librarianship. In many universities, librarians have transitioned from being perceived as one-dimensional staff to having faculty status, where they not only teach credit-bearing classes but also serve on committees and publish within the field. Dig through your local archives long enough and you may be lucky enough to find mimeographed handouts or slides from early instruction sessions. In our technological age, it can be easy to laugh at how far we have come in our instruction, but look closely at what we were teaching then and you will see that the content has changed very little. Still, if the content is fundamentally the same, why are we still discussing library instruction? Put simply, our methodologies and ways of presenting change constantly, and what makes information literacy so refreshing is that we have the ability to assess what we have done and make purposeful changes if necessary.

List of Alternate Job Titles for Instruction Coordinators

Blended Librarian

Coordinator of Library Instruction

Head of Instructional Services

Information Literacy Coordinator

Information Services Librarian

Instruction Schedule Coordinator

Instructional Designer

Critical Research Instruction Librarian

Teaching and Learning Program Librarian

Training Librarian

_____ (Your Title Here)

Critically, instruction coordinators often act as sounding boards for instruction librarians looking for support and guidance as they go about their information literacy path. This might mean that you will be perceived more as a superior than a friend, but during times of crisis and tough love, you need to act as a leader for your team. Find the overall path for your team's instruction. How does the English 101 session help guide students in the Philosophy capstone project? Instruction coordinators bring out the joy in instruction and help guide others toward their best moments in the classroom. Frequently, when librarians become fed up with instruction, their frustration comes not from students in the classroom or even the act of teaching itself but from demands outside the classroom that affect how they teach or are asked to teach. Sometimes it comes from new assessment measures in the curricula.

Who Coordinates?

Who are the instruction coordinators in the library? Are they just library instructors who have taken on a little more power, or are they something else? As I began my research into the world of instruction coordination, I began to notice patterns in what types of people were drawn to the role and who stayed. My first surprise was in discovering that most of my survey respondents were relatively new to the role, many having only been in the position for three or fewer years. The number of people who had been in the role longer than ten years was relatively small. In part, this could reflect the fact that the position terminology has been a recent development, but even taking title changes into account, the majority of the survey responses came from those new to the role. This is not meant to imply that these people lacked library experience; indeed, many had years of experience as instruction librarians prior to transitioning into their current roles. A common conception of the profession is that it is white female dominated. Certainly, the number of female librarians hovers around 82 percent, and the number of white librarians is similar, but as the ALA Office for Diversity, Literacy, and Outreach Services shows, we are trying to fix this issue to make the field more approachable to others.[1] And we aim to diversify not just who we are but how we perform the work of librarianship. Being an instruction coordinator means being aware of and reflecting on the field's trends and how your own particular institution can and should react to them.

Criticism

Coordinator roles run amok in the world of librarianship. The term *coordinator* frequently refers to any functional role with some level of management and oversight. The name can be so vague as to promote a lack of understanding of what exactly a coordinator is other than the tautological "one who coordinates." Indeed, the stress on coordination places a lot of emphasis on the managerial aspects of the job and less on the core duties that may preface the role. Library job titles change periodically not only to better reflect the specific roles but also to make the roles clearer to the public. For a long time, most of us only had the most basic title: librarian. Today, there are many flavors of librarian, and when we create new roles or reimagine new titles for old positions, it's important to think about what those titles convey and what we focus on. The newest way of thinking about librarian roles is that we tend to fall into the two different categories of functional versus specialist librarians (Jaguszweski and Williams 2013). Regardless of what your specific title is right now or how it may be rewritten in the future, this book focuses on the specific role of the person who manages instruction as well as the needs of that instruction. It's a function that needs to be served, whether by faculty, staff, or even, in some cases, student aides. Whether or not it is a supervisory role, a strategic organizational schema must be in place to ensure that instruction is brought on.

Purpose

Although you can certainly find yourself thrown into a new title like instruction coordinator and make a strong go of it, in order to figure out just what is expected of you and how to fulfill those desires, it is handy to have something to lean on for guidance. With that in mind, this book offers worksheets, tips, and best practices for those who are new to the role and those who might be experiencing burnout and are looking for something new to revive their approach to the role.

In fact, if you are looking for ideas about how to refresh individual instruction or be a better one-shot teacher or just need lesson plans, that information is not hard to find. Go to Twitter, look through library-oriented blogs, and attend conference sessions and you will walk away with plenty of inspiring ideas. Coming up with ideas is rarely a struggle, but there is a surprising lack of detailed examples of how to be an instruction coordinator. The role combines managerial skills and instructional skills in a unique intersection that few address. It is worth taking a thoughtful and considered approach to how you fill these shoes, especially if you want to build a successful program.

Exciting times are afoot in information literacy. As of this writing, the Association of College and Research Libraries (ACRL) Information Literacy standards—not just a threshold to the field but in some ways perhaps the scaffolding of our thought patterns—have recently been revised into the new Framework for Information Literacy in Higher Education. Because it is so recent, the field as a whole will need some time to interpret and apply it to our work. This could be reflected in our assessment or our practices, but most importantly, not only do instruction coordinators need to read these materials, but they also need to help their instructors interpret the new framework—or any material that comes along during their tenure.

Framework Sandbox: Check out the ACRL Framework Information Literacy Sandbox to find resources and help you better understand the framework: http://sandbox.acrl.org.

As an instructor you have probably spent your time teaching one-shots to students and are very good at it, but as a coordinator, your role has changed, and now it is time to understand how things work behind the curtain. For a long time, I simplified my language when asked what I did for a living and referred to myself as just "a librarian," which led to confusion, as people assumed I worked for the county library or otherwise. In recent years, I have begun to reclaim my title, and I introduce myself as an instruction coordinator, which has led to an uptick in prolonged questions about what I do. I encourage you to move out into the open about your job. The longer we hide behind our generic titles, the longer people remain in the dark about what an instruction coordinator does. We do exciting work that's worth talking about, so let's share it. In a field that has historically been marketed toward women and has been built on the gendered idea of passivity, let's speak up, lead, and celebrate!

Overview

Each chapter in this book is focused on unique areas of an instruction coordinator's day-to-day life. Of specific interest is the academic calendar in chapter 5. This generalized academic calendar focuses less on specific drop dates and commencements for the university and more on the particular instruction hurdles that arise on a fairly predictable schedule for most librarians. Indeed, most chapters will include real-world worksheets and handouts that have proven to be useful for both managing the workflow of an instruction librarian and planning simple classroom exercises and lessons.

NOTE

1.   American Library Association, "Diversity Counts 2009–2010 Update,"
     ALA Office for Diversity, 2012, www.ala.org/offices/diversity/
     diversitycounts/2009-2010update/.

FURTHER READINGS

ACRL Information Literacy Competency Standards for Higher Education Task Force.
    "Framework for Information Literacy in Higher Education." 2015. www.ala.org/
    acrl/standards/ilframework/.

American Library Association. "Diversity Counts 2009–2010 Update." ALA Office for
    Diversity. 2012. www.ala.org/offices/diversity/diversitycounts/2009-
    2010update/.

Booth, Char. *Reflective Teaching, Effective Learning: Instructional Literacy for Library
    Educators.* Chicago: ALA Editions of the American Library Association, 2011.

Grassian, Esther S., and Joan R. Kaplowitz. *Learning to Lead and Manage Information
    Literacy Instruction.* New York: Neal-Schuman, 2005.

Jaguszewski, J. and Karen Williams. "New Roles for New Times: Transforming
    Liaison Roles in Research Libraries." Association of Research Libraries, 2013.

2

People

Introduction

The very nature of working as an instruction coordinator guarantees near daily interaction with people. For the extrovert, what a joy! And for the introvert, what a challenge! This chapter looks at the various groups of people an instruction coordinator will come in contact with and covers specifically how to deal with these differing groups, as each can require a different approach and have different needs. People who are drawn to instruction tend to be customer service oriented, which will help in the long run, but as a coordinator, you will need to draw a line as to what is appropriate to give.

One of the first things I realized as I began work on this project was how relational the work of being an instruction coordinator can be. It requires and relies on a good deal of building and maintaining effective relationships. Sometimes the fruits of these relationships will take years to pan out, but a good coordinator finds the ways to not only sell their program, but find the needs of their campus. In this chapter, we will also look at how specific communities and relationships can be strengthened and used in the context of being an instruction coordinator. Many coordinators spoke of their relationships with professors and students as one of the best aspects of their job, not least because it granted them the opportunity to help students one-on-one and see how truly effective their instruction could be. The ability to see clear results can motivate and reinvigorate your work.

Much of the work discussed in this chapter falls under the broad category of networking. For some, this work can be a natural extension of their personas, and for others it can feel like, well, work.[1] Networking takes on many adaptive, unique aspects of the fields it is applied to; what works for one field may not apply to others. A great number of resources focus solely on networking; within this work, we will reflect more on how instruction coordinators can apply networking techniques to get what they need.

Speaking of, what counts as networking? You might be surprised. For starters, listening to people—seriously. Do not listen to others waiting to interject with your fabulous rebuttal or point. Do not spend the majority of the time thinking about your own response; just listen to what they have to say. When groups feel heard and understood, half the battle is won. It is your job to listen to what these groups need and apply your own sense of what library instruction can actually offer in return. Similarly, try not to think of the library and instruction as institutions that only give. Look for ways that partnerships can return goodness to the library through either programming or joint ventures that meet both of your needs. What do other departments need and how can instruction help meet those needs?

Faculty

Throughout this chapter and the book, faculty are referred to as teaching faculty or content professors, and this is done for a few distinctive reasons. First and foremost, this is to distinguish between faculty who teach semester-long classes in one core subject from library faculty. Another distinction is nine-month-contract faculty versus twelve-month-contract faculty. Although not all academic libraries offer faculty status to their librarians, increasingly more librarians find themselves members of the faculty body. With this increase in faculty status comes an awareness of how wildly our jobs can vary from the standard teaching faculty's role, so when referencing such faculty, I want to be clear I am referring to faculty who are not librarians and may be unfamiliar with library norms. Although there have been many contentious discussions regarding whether or not librarians should be given faculty status, in this book, I assume most academic librarians reading this have some form of faculty status. Second, due to the nature of our roles within the institution, librarians are teachers, and there are many ways to refer to us. We are librarians, yes, but we are also teachers, faculty, professors, and instructors. Many librarians do not come from an educational background where they have been trained in classroom management or pedagogy, and it can be difficult to fully embrace a word such as teacher when we feel we are not fully equipped with pedagogical knowledge or dispositions. While more library schools are adapting their curriculum to help with library instruction, it has not been historically the norm. I think we can only strengthen ourselves by aligning with stronger pedagogy and an assertion of who we are—teachers. With all these varied terms, it is welcoming to have a standardized word to use in this book so that we know who is who. This is not meant in any way to give deference to one particular group over another; it is simply a way of demarcating the differences between two very similar groups.

Teaching faculty and instruction librarians must engage in interprofessional collaboration. Information literacy as a practice has been lurking around for some time. As information literacy becomes less of a new concept to teaching faculty, our methods also need to change to keep things fresh and make sure that targets do not become obscured by the ways things have always been done. Some librarians have applied relationship models to librarian-faculty relationships to analyze what makes specific relationships flourish and, just as important, what hinders the growth of these relationships.[2] Sometimes these relationships were analyzed by Myers-Briggs Type Indicator; other contributors were things such as shared values, opportunism, and communication. It is important to consider what values we share, specifically because they will be called into play during times of crisis or unrest. If this should seem unnecessarily dark, remember that most teaching faculty and librarians interact minimally throughout the semester. When not teaching information literacy sessions for them, we often fall back in their consciousness only to reappear should there be a collection development issue or specific funding crisis. As Phelps and Campbell put it, "It is clear that the importance of the relationship is primarily to librarians" (17). This cannot be stressed enough for librarians who desire to create a strong relationship with teaching faculty. Since the relationship between the two groups appears to be of a higher importance to librarians, the onus falls on us to find ways to maintain the relationship; encourage teaching faculty to bring their classes into the library; and most importantly, help create a long-term collaboration between teaching faculty and the library.

Typically, an instruction coordinator can embrace outreach by attending the start-of-year department meetings for the core subjects they are looking to engage with. Sometimes subject bibliographers are the natural allies to come to these meetings. Who comes to represent the library is flexible, but getting people in the door is crucial. One cannot and should not expect to be given much time during these meetings to promote library services. One tactic that provides a twist on the usual format of reminding teaching faculty of new resources and services they may want to take advantage of is to come with a prepared lesson that can easily be dropped into the subjects' information literacy plans. Be sure to connect the lesson with standards or goals that the teaching faculty may be trying to hit with their own lesson plans. If this seems like a tall order, think about ways that you can break this up into manageable tasks.

Sample Activities

One year, I decided to prepare a lesson plan that could be dropped into any English 101 class. Using YouTube videos on how to make pizza, I found three sources that ranged in quality from good to comically bad (the comically bad having been filmed by us). Students were asked to view these videos before the library session and submit a short response on which video was the most authoritative and why. This allowed me to immediately begin a discussion on authority as soon as class began.

I presented this lesson to English composition faculty at their start-of-year meeting and had success: more than three faculty members chose to use it in class.

In some respects, this may involve research into association standards and discussions with teaching faculty about what they are trying to accomplish when they teach their own students. During these discussions, try not to interject with places where information literacy could be applied—or at least not immediately. Rather, use it as a fact-finding mission to both gather and gain goodwill and learn what teaching faculty are working toward and how information literacy can aid those specific goals. Part of why this method works so well is that teaching faculty may indeed want to teach toward their specific standards or bring them into the library, but they fail to see ways to incorporate these ideas themselves. Offering ideas and plans that can easily be adapted by the teaching faculty gives them an easy way to approach the library and teach these lessons. In addition, most teaching faculty do not think of the library until the start of the semester. Your physical presence acts as a reminder to those who may not naturally remember information literacy until the last minute.

There are pitfalls to this plan. Teaching faculty may not see the value in the lesson plans an instruction coordinator brings forward, or spending five or ten minutes at a departmental meeting may not be the best way to gain access to your specific institution's teaching faculty. Each institution has its own unique interpersonal relations, and it is worth being aware of your own institutional climate before implementing a new change or method. Another problem with presenting during these meetings is that having such a short time to present forces you to limit how much you can say. Much of the talk may be limited to simply giving handouts and brochures. Still the point of these activities involves a long game of library recognition. Just as some may be turned off by canned lesson plans and handouts, others see a relief for a gap in their syllabus they didn't know how to feel, or a reminder to reach out to someone they previously hadn't known how to.

Many instruction programs now specifically provide an "instruction menu" in order to give teaching faculty a clearer idea of what they can offer.[3] The concept focuses on providing teaching faculty distinct options from a preset list. While some teaching faculty approach the library beforehand with an expectation of how the class is to be taught, some only have a vague notion. Having a menu can help some teaching faculty grasp the idea of information literacy without offering a prescriptive lesson plan. Similarly, this often can serve as a way to introduce concepts that faculty were unaware that librarians could do. Particularly with services surrounding copyright, open access and other areas that may not be seen as traditional library subjects. As with all lesson planning options, some librarians have noted a fault with this method: teaching faculty might begin to believe that the options on the menu are the only options they can choose from, and if those options do not meet their needs, they feel there might not be any specific information literacy options for them. However, the strength of the menu is that it allows an information literacy program to highlight specific resources and tools that may not get covered in class as often. A sample menu approach allows teaching faculty to go to a webpage and select specific lesson plans or items they would like their students to learn, and it also prevents them from requesting that too many skills be taught at one time.

Sample Menu

1. How to use citations
2. Using newspaper sources and historic materials
3. How to find articles
4. How to identify key terms
5. Discuss Open Access and Copyright Issues
6. Discuss Digital Privacy
7. Library tour

Librarians

Considering that the majority of the people instruction coordinators work with from day to day are librarians, there is value in making sure that those who do *not* work in instruction fully understand the work and function of instruction and information literacy. Although it is unlikely that any institution performing instruction would have librarians unfamiliar with the concept, the details of how that instruction is performed may be fuzzier for people who are not actively engaged in the work. Just as instruction librarians may be unfamiliar with the minutiae of a cataloger's day-to-day work, do not make assumptions that everyone fundamentally understands the nature of instruction. Note that if you are part of a liaison structured environment, all liaisons should ideally be doing some amount of instruction.

Particularly if tenure-track librarians are part of the instruction team, the instruction coordinator must act as a conduit for other librarians during the tenure process to let them know the value of presenting at certain conferences or how to interpret different aspects of the classroom instruction experience. Instruction coordinators certainly deal with many day-to-day aspects of scheduling and making sure that content is covered, but some of the larger-scale institution-wide needs involve ensuring that librarians will want to stay and helping them stay by acting as a guide through the tenure process. Tenure varies across institution types, including its duration and the specifics needed to gain it. Some institutions are more rigorous than others, but in general, the needs reflect what the library offers to its student population. Generally, a library instructor going up for tenure will need a variety of research-level articles and publications in addition to presentations and service on local and national organizations. It is not a small feat, and the service and professional development opportunities needed for tenure can frequently take a person away from instruction at inopportune times. Use your position to ensure that the people on the tenure committee are aware of just how important the work of the instruction team is. And be sure committee members who are not involved with instruction understand why a conference on instruction would be viewed well within the community or how much work might go into a particular assessment project. Similarly, if you feel comfortable, acting as a mentor to those untenured instruction librarians can help tremendously if you feel that you know what specific facets of instruction will appeal to a tenure committee. The instruction coordinator role is often well placed to act as mentor for tenure track librarians.

A final word on tenure: Tenure is a massive issue for working academic librarians today. Not all academic librarians are granted tenure or even given the option to work through it, and of those who are, the strictures under which it is granted can vary vastly.[4] Some libraries have a similar tenure process, with continuous employment being granted. Others give faculty status but not tenure, and the process for all of this can be just as rigorous. As a group, librarians have a lot of mixed feelings about their faculty status.[5] Some of this debate rests on the shoulders of our terminal degree: the masters of library science (MLS) or information science. People argue that without a PhD, we cannot call ourselves faculty, and others argue that an MLS is our terminal degree and just as valid. Although instruction coordinators typically do not have a great deal of influence over these decisions, they can help tenure-track librarians learn how to present their instruction-based items within the university's professional requirements. When library instruction is presented to the greater university tenure committee, the information can often seem at odds with the type of instruction that most teaching faculty are used to. Their evaluations come once a semester; ours can come after each session. Their course products can be syllabi and long-term tests and assignments; ours are frequently items like before and after exams. To say that there are major differences is almost an understatement.

Librarians such as vanDuinkerken, Coker, and Anderson[6] have made the argument that tenure packages should leave out instruction materials just to avoid confusing teaching faculty. When considering what to add to a tenure package, every little thing counts. Although the instruction coordinator does not have a final say on who in their department gets tenure, if you have already gone through the process, you can help prepare a newer librarian by discussing what materials are important to save and how to highlight important works and best practices. For those new to the tenure process, this advice can be invaluable.

With information literacy, there is also a growing belief that everything done in the library is a form of information literacy. Yes, this makes intuitive sense, but older models such as Christine Bruce's[7] and Shirley Behrens's[8] often look at information literacy through the scope of an action solely related to library research, whereas the modern framework holds that information literacy is a lifelong learning process. There are different tactics to use here as an instruction coordinator. The first step is to define information literacy for yourself and what that means in terms of who teaches it. Is it solely taught by librarians? Can professional staff participate in some way? What about embedded and online instruction? The pandemic has taught us that instruction can take place over many modalities, but often needs to have accommodations of many types. Defining the boundaries of your collaborations and instruction sessions gives you the ability not only to determine how information literacy is presented to the university at large but also to conscientiously give students and staff a consistent message. Finally, knowing your instruction programs boundaries, gives *you* greater understanding for how to lead the program.

My Information Literacy Goals

Information literacy is taught by . . .

_____

Information literacy covers . . .

_____

Information literacy applies to . . .

_____

In part, defining who is an instructor may mean that people who typically do not perceive themselves as instructors become so. If an archivist is asked to begin teaching information literacy, what does that look like? The Society of American Archivists has their own take on information literacy, and while they have significant overlap with Association of College and Research Libraries' (ACRL's) viewpoints, they take their own archival approach[9] that focuses much more on primary source material and developing critical thought while also finding a balance with providing access. Even pedagogical methods of lecture versus group discussion may differ. The clearer your image of information literacy, the easier it is to perform. It is difficult to stress how simple yet wickedly complex the concept is. When the idea becomes muddled in the minds of others, lots of people will be stakeholders, but their investment will vary greatly, and indeed, their image of information literacy might differ so wildly from yours that you could both equally believe you are teaching information literacy and be teaching radically different ideas. Part of the problem is that information literacy is an incredibly flexible topic that can apply to many different areas of life, so there is a natural assumption that because you are doing the same thing in one area, it is reflected in another or needs no differentiating. Having a consistent message to refer back to can help each group understand how to get information literacy across. I prefer to think of information literacy as the umbrella under which there are manifold types of literacies. There is data literacy, visual literacy, mathematics literacy, and so on, and information literacy applies to all these areas, but the techniques used for each will vary slightly. Creating a definition that works for you can encourage and give shape and modality to how you view your own lesson planning. When it comes to introducing information literacy, the default is to frame the concept of credibility as a binary, in which information is either good or bad. Although there are certainly resources and information that would be bad in specific situations, it is critical for students to understand that information literacy is about finding the right information for the right scenario; just because some information is not relevant to their research needs does not necessarily mean it is "bad." A good way to convey the idea is to focus on the phrase "affirmation is not information." Many students begin their research with a preconceived idea of what type of information they are looking for. It is important to stress to them that just because they have a belief or understanding of what is true, there is value in looking at all sides of the truth.

Administration

The instruction coordinator will regularly deal with two levels of administration: the library dean or head librarian that an instruction coordinator directly reports to and the university administration, which may not often have a direct influence on the work of instruction librarians but will certainly have indirect ramifications on his or her work based on varying institutional goals at the time. During restructuring years, instruction coordinators might need to rethink how they address instruction in certain core classes or perhaps even target other areas of instruction. If the university encourages you to participate in faculty governance for rank and tenure, then there is a very high chance that you will be involved with some level of administration during committee work. It can be tempting to think that since you do not have regularly held semester-long courses, these issues do not affect you or the library, but this is an incredibly short-sighted way to view these decisions. The university ecosystem is similar to that of a pond or lake. Things that happen on the other side of the pond will eventually contaminate the water or ripple their way over to your portion of the pond. Though the actions taken may not directly affect you, at some point they likely will have ramifications for you or your library colleagues. Being aware of such things enables you to prepare and know what ripple effects are coming down the line for the library. Consider also the university strategic plan and how it applies at a granular level to the instruction that you do on the ground. Strategic plans often have high level concepts, but they are intended to be used in the very specific world of how we interact with our students. Instruction coordinators should listen for the intent of these strategic plans and see how they apply to their specific programs.

Library administrators are the people you will see on a near daily or weekly basis. Administration varies by personality type, naturally, but generally speaking, the core elements they will want from you are statistics and assessment data they can bring forward in reports and grants, and the instruction coordinator should focus on replying with timely and accurate information. Since these measures are used for a lot of resources, try not to prejudge what they could be for. Sometimes you will know ahead of time why administrators are requesting this information, but at other times, it is not your place to know, and that's fine. Generally, they need the information to find funding for programs, arrange greater services, and create reports. Sometimes, when libraries are going through renovation, administrators will need input from people who use the spaces daily. As an instruction coordinator, you may be asked how the computer labs and classrooms are used and must be aware of what they require and how they are not working. Spaces might simply need new furniture, or they might have structural needs, such as more power outlets, better lighting, and so on. Regardless, the administration needs your input when making decisions about renovations and, importantly, budgeting for those renovations.

Budget lines are another major issue of concern. While not all instruction coordinators have a dedicated budget line for instruction, many have at least a small token amount that can be used toward gift incentives or marketing. Sometimes these budget lines will be portioned out of departmental budgets, and other times they come out of ancillary lines, but they are important to demarcate as different from the needs of reference or public services. Keeping in touch with the administration will help you understand what counts as acceptable use as well as provide feedback on your instruction librarians' needs. Many times librarians like to use these small lines for things like candy for large orientations or library-branded swag like pens, erasers, and so on. Although these are small purchases, they do add up—especially when distributed to the entire freshman class—and the coordinator will need to show that the money is being used responsibly. Certainly, if the line is not meeting your needs and you find that either you or your librarians are making purchases out of pocket, this issue needs to be addressed with administrators. Money is a tough subject for many people to feel comfortable discussing, particularly with those that they may not be on close terms with the ones they speak with or particularly when talking to those who have seniority to them. I urge you to face these meetings head on when appropriate by bringing to the forefront the areas you may feel uncomfortable with or need a little more guidance on. In addition, use these meetings with administration not only to address departmental issues but also to ask for help with the line. If you do not have a budget line, consider asking for one. Some libraries have very small lines of only $100 a year, and some have more robust lines, but these are small bids to open with. One question that can come up is how to figure out the department's repeated budgetary needs. Academic years can be extremely repetitive, and yearly variances and inflation can create the need to establish check-in points for these budgets. First, confirm what money is solely related to instruction and what is tangentially related to other services that perhaps can come from other lines, such as professional development or library-wide marketing services. Sometimes it can help to go through the instruction calendar and look at the details for past events, especially if it would be useful to see what items were purchased for specific classes. If your past experience has only been with personal budgeting, familiarize yourself with what a professional budget request looks like and the standard practice for presenting these requests. Incentives typically work best with lower-level classes, so if more lower-level than upper-division classes are being taught, this can affect what purchases are made.

TABLE 2.1
Sample budget line

Projected	Actual budgeted
AV equipment	
Continuing education	
E-books	
Discretionary	

Patron Incentives

In addition to monetary concerns, frequently instruction coordinators may need to seek approval for larger overarching themes that instruction deals with. Particularly when it comes to frustrations with certain departments or outside faculty members, a library dean may be better placed to help smooth over the situation and make sure that everyone walks away with at least some of their needs met. For example, when trouble arises with other groups on campus, it can be incredibly tempting to take issues personally and respond quickly in the heat of the moment. However, before rushing to click "Send" on an ill-thought-out reply, it helps to at least pause and vet the situation before the dean to get a sense of his or her preferred tactic. In some cases, instruction coordinators have even drafted responses and coedited them with their deans in order to present a united front when confronting a particularly thorny issue, such as discontent during an instruction session, technology failures, or why you are refusing to offer instruction to certain classes again. The longer you work with the administration, the better you will know their preferred styles and when they want to hear from you. It takes time to develop these relationships, but in the long haul, it can be worth it.

Students

One of the stranger thought processes when it comes to interactions with students on our campuses is to assume that only our direct work with students in classrooms matters. It is an interesting concept to consider, because instruction librarians—even embedded librarians—only have a limited amount of face time with students. It would be easy to assume that thus we have only a small impact on their day-to-day lives. Not so! We affect students in thousands of microtransactions every day. Every facet of our service to students, from the library web page to the type of furniture and its layout, effects how they think about librarians and the library. These tiny day-to-day transactions affect the decisions students will make about whether they want to come into the library to study for a midterm or even the simple matter of whether they perceive a library instruction class to be worth their time or something they can skip. Battling these perceptions means finding ways that we can improve the overall experience for students entering the library.

As a coordinator, certainly you will engage with students in the classroom, but there are other avenues for engaging with students that can help you discover how to be a better instructor and ensure that the work of information literacy is not falling on deaf ears. Creative ways to engage with students can vary by both the type of student and your own metric. However, many find it easier to approach a student who is more familiar to them. Most libraries have a wealth of information available in student employees who help out at service desks and within acquisition areas. Student employees can offer insights into what they perceive they need from the library. Of course, a major caveat is that students who choose to work in a library may view libraries in a more positive light than other students or might simply be affected by the inherent power dynamics. This is not to say that all their information or words should be discredited, but use your own best judgment to determine when their feelings are genuine, when they are fawning, and when to look for other viewpoints. These students can even refer you to other friends who may be more forthcoming and honest about their views on the library. More importantly, when you engage with student workers beyond the basics of point-of-need interactions, you gain a greater perspective of what student life is like at your university. Even if your perspective is not vastly changed, this information can inform how lessons are planned and administered. Ultimately, decisions based on known facts rather than presumed feelings are better decisions.

Student panels and focus groups can provide insights that go beyond librarian perspectives and can offer advice that may be unexpected or hard to hear. Although few instructors go into teaching with the attitude that every student they reach will be radically transformed by their instruction, most instructors go in with at least the hope that they are having some small effect on learning and helping. With student panels, we can create questions to find desired outcomes, but frequently we craft these questions expecting specific replies from students. It is very hard to overcome this bias. On the other hand, when we ask students extremely open-ended questions, they may not know where to start or give simple answers because they lack a framework to guide them. One way to get around these obstacles is to structure a meeting around one specific question, spend the majority of the time listening to students discuss their thoughts on that topic, and then respond with directed questions on how these issues can be resolved. Are there some optional "This would be nice but isn't needed" items versus those that would absolutely be deal breakers? Listening can help focus the conversation without making the library appear one-sided, assaulting students with questions.

The Public at Large

Attitudes and expectations toward working with the public at large vary wildly from institution to institution. If your institution is a state university or classified as a federal depository by the Government Printing Office, there might be slightly different regulations on how you work with the public. Private institutions, on the other hand, are frequently free to impose their own boundaries on how they interact with the public. However, defining "the public" is a very tricky subject. Your first impulse may be to think of community users who come into the library to use computers or the collections without a direct affiliation with the university. They are certainly a large portion of the public, but there are other contingencies to consider. For example, think about your interactions with others when you are *not* at work. People will often ask what you do or what is new at the library, and they may even ask for specifics on gossip about other factions of the university. If your institution happens to have a high number of graduates who stay in the area, you might find yourself frequently discussing these matters with alumni of multiple generations. For a certain number of people, it is still uncommon to hear about librarians teaching. As an instruction coordinator, part of the work is to make information literacy instruction more commonly understood and recognized, particularly considering that the attitudes of alumni can affect us, often in unseen ways. Donors are certainly a contingent to be aware of, but think also of their own children, who may someday choose to come to the same school. The more we can make these people aware of what a sea change and transition librarians have undergone, the more acceptable we can make information literacy to the masses. Going into details and specifics may be the way for you, but as you partner more with faculty and outside departments across campus, you may find you have a better ability to communicate the new abilities of librarians through demonstration rather than explanation.

For myself, I always found the ACRL Framework to be a difficult concept to explain to people who were not linked to academia in some way, but as I began to structure my sessions around it, I noticed that it became easier to explain to others because I was able to use concrete examples. Instead of telling a friend that I was working on the "Authority Is Constructed and Con-textual" frame, I could point out how I had my students create Wikipedia articles by making them research and fact-check everything they put up on the site for stub articles. Using this as an entry point for people who might not be familiar with the more detailed aspects of our work can draw others into a larger conversation and give them a toehold onto deeper perspectives in the field. When you have concrete examples to offer people outside of the academic system, they can often find a way to understand the concept and even leverage what you offer them into future partnerships. This is particu-larly useful for departments on campus that may not have a regular student body, like offices for transferring students or honors students, and instead those in student engagement may see ways to leverage library instruction into unique activities that can bring wider buy-in across campus.

A counterargument to the above is that this is the work of administra-tion and not our specific battle-ax. Particularly for those of us who may not be salaried and are only paid hourly, it can be difficult to motivate ourselves to continue our work when we are not on the clock, and perhaps from an equality standpoint, you may be unwilling to take on the burden. However, if you feel capable of taking this work outside the office, there are a few bul-let points you may want to hit. For example, stick to points about the library that you fully understand. If you do not have experience in a particular area of the library, it is more than OK to tell a stranger that that is not your area of expertise, but do feel welcome to redirect with topics that you are more com-fortable with and excited to share. This type of networking is easy to jump into because it involves sharing.

Many libraries offer instruction to groups outside of their own specific institution. Many libraries are eager to provide instructions to classes from local high schools, where a teacher may be introducing their students to the broader concept of academic research and trying to open their minds to the greater world of academia beyond high school. Although the instruction in these classes may be limited by what resources outsiders from the univer-sity have access to, it often relies on the very fundamental roots of infor-mation literacy. Teaching such classes is a great outreach moment for any library, and as an instruction coordinator, you should prepare those teaching the class for how it differs from a typical class. Many times when these out-side classes come into the university, they bring their own expectations about what a library is. This can be a great learning moment for people to learn the differences between the historical stereotype of a library and the modern library. For example, the scene I have witnessed time and again is a group of high schoolers, exuberant and jovial, walking into the library and then immediately shushing one another. The scene can be cute to witness, but it is a great point to bring up that the presumption of all-enveloping silence within the library walls is frequently no longer entirely accurate in most libraries.

Working with School Groups

Bringing information literacy into a one-shot session with students who may not be able to use your databases or the majority of your collection can seem difficult, but it is possible, and sometimes there are even more options than normal!

- Consider reaching out to the school librarian or media center specialist to see what objectives they are reaching for that year.
- Often teachers bring classes in for a specific local project or research beyond their collection. Offer students a chance to discuss issues with access to information.
- Many students will have never been in a library as big as yours and may be unfamiliar with research scholarship. Strategically using items from the special collections or archives can help make the experience feel special while promoting items from your own collection.
- Activities are essential, especially when students don't have a strong assignment beyond a basic tour. Options such as Observe and Report, Thematic Collect and Interpret, and simplified Google Hunts can all be fun for students.

One specific thing to observe is how you refer to local student groups and your own students at the college. When we speak about students, either to their faces or indirectly, as "kids," "kiddos," "youths," or any number of diminutive terms, we do them a real disservice. When we use such diminutives, we place them at a lower pedestal. In our culture, we have different expectations for children than we do for adults, and when we teach students about information literacy, we must do it from a level playing field rather than from a place of condescension. I urge you to think of this not just as an age-related factor but also on a spectrum of knowledge. Think of it as introducing students to a mutual level of respect. Some librarians feel a level of superiority and look down on freshman and lower-level undergraduates when they think about their research skills. Just as we must be careful not to demean students based on age, we must also take each student at his or her own educational level. Students are not "dumb" or "stupid" because they happen to be oblivious to things that we know to be obvious or true. Most librarians have multiple college degrees, and students usually do not. They are new to this process that is old to us. They are sometimes ignorant, but fixing that is the work of information literacy. This applies when you are considering whether to teach a higher-level concept—thinking, "Will students be interested in this?"—just as much as when you talk about students at conferences. Offering our respect through simple language readjustments creates a welcoming environment that students want to participate in. Creating unnecessary barriers only hurts the instruction program as a whole. The instruction coordinator can help create a culture of inclusion rather than exclusion by paying attention to how instructors talk about students both when they are present and when they are not. Check your assumptions and know your student population.

Summary

Instruction librarians tend to like interacting with different groups on campus, and the instruction coordinator comes into contact with more groups than most. Knowing how to navigate the demands and needs of each of these unique populations puts the instruction coordinator at an advantage for promoting information literacy across the campus. It will take time to develop meaningful relationships with some groups, but positive interactions will speed up the process.

Worksheets and Activities

Instruction coordinators can use the Faculty Profile form (figure 2.1) to remember specifics about each teaching faculty member. This is particularly helpful at an institution with a large faculty or high turnover. "Known issues" can refer to anything a new instructor may want to know about the teaching faculty member, such as that they may use the library session as babysitting or that they like to use a specific assignment style.

FIGURE 2.1
Faculty profile

Name:

Email:

Phone number:

Area of interest:

Courses taught:

____ Active

____ Nonactive

Associated librarians:

      (Names of any librarians who have taught classes for the professor)

Known issues:

Notes:

Collect-and-Interpret Activities

When professors ask for a scavenger hunt in the library, it can be tempting to immediately roll your eyes, especially as these activities frequently fill time but do not add anything meaningful to the learning process.

    Collect-and-interpret activities can meet the scavenger hunt request but reinterpret it to add an educational element.

- Have students gather books and items on several specific topics (one topic per group).

- When they are reunited in class, have students discuss why the books were arranged in the way they were, why they were not in a related area, or why books gathered from two different areas would be separated.

NOTES

1. H. Wolff and S. Kim, "The Relationship between Networking Behaviors and the Big Five Personality Dimensions," *Career Development International* 17, no. 1 (2012): 43–66.
2. Sue F. Phelps and Nicole Campbell, "Commitment and Trust in Librarian–Faculty Relationships: A Systematic Review of the Literature," *Journal of Academic Librarianship* 38, no. 1 (2012): 13–19.
3. Candice Benjes-Small and Blair Brainard, "And Today We'll Be Serving: An Instruction a la Carte Menu," *College and Research Libraries News* 67, no. 2 (2006).
4. J. M. Welch and F. L. Mozenter, "Loosening the Ties That Bind: Academic Librarians and Tenure," *College and Research Libraries* 67, no. 2 (2006): 164–76.
5. B. H. Danielle, "Faculty Status for Librarians in Higher Education," *portal: Libraries and the Academy* 3, no. 3 (2003): 431–45.
6. Wyoma vanDuinkerken, Catherine Coker, and Margaret Anderson, "Looking like Everyone Else: Academic Portfolios for Librarians," *Journal of Academic Librarianship* 36, no. 2 (2010): 166–72.
7. C. S. Bruce, *Seven Faces of Information Literacy* (Adelaide: Auslib Press, 1997).
8. S. J. Behrens, "A Conceptual Analysis and Historical Overview of Information Literacy," *College and Research Libraries* 55, no. 2 (1994): 309–22.
9. Elizabeth Yakel, "Information Literacy for Primary Sources: Creating a New Paradigm for Archival Researcher Education," *OCLC Systems and Services: International Digital Library Perspectives* 20, no. 2 (2004): 61–64.

FURTHER READINGS

Behrens, S. J. "A Conceptual Analysis and Historical Overview of Information Literacy." *College and Research Libraries* 55, no. 2 (1994): 309–22.

Benjes-Small, Candice, and Blair Brainard. "And Today We'll Be Serving: An Instruction a La Carte Menu." *College and Research Libraries News* 67, no. 2 (2006).

Bruce, C. S. *Seven Faces of Information Literacy.* Adelaide: Auslib Press, 1997.

Danielle, B. H. "Faculty Status for Librarians in Higher Education." *portal: Libraries and the Academy* 3, no. 3 (2003): 431–45.

Phelps, Sue F., and Nicole Campbell. "Commitment and Trust in Librarian–Faculty Relationships: A Systematic Review of the Literature." *Journal of Academic Librarianship* 38, no. 1 (2012): 13–19.

vanDuinkerken, Wyoma, Catherine Coker, and Margaret Anderson. "Looking like Everyone Else: Academic Portfolios for Librarians." *Journal of Academic Librarianship* 36, no. 2 (2010): 166–72.

Welch, J. M., and F. L. Mozenter. "Loosening the Ties That Bind: Academic Librarians and Tenure." *College and Research Libraries* 67, no. 2 (2006): 164–76.

Wolff, H., and S. Kim. "The Relationship between Networking Behaviors and the Big Five Personality Dimensions." *Career Development International* 17, no. 1 (2012): 43–66.

Yakel, Elizabeth. "Information Literacy for Primary Sources: Creating a New Paradigm for Archival Researcher Education." *OCLC Systems and Services: International Digital Library Perspectives* 20, no. 2 (2004): 61–64.

3

Training

Introduction

Training your instruction librarians how to work at the library and use the systems in place takes time and ongoing methods, as well as a well-thought-out process of what is working and what is not. This chapter deals with some topics that should be addressed by a functional workshop, including techniques, reflection, and new methods. Use it as a point of reference for ideas and ways to help lead and manage a workshop. This is intended as a pick-up-and-go chapter for ideas on ways to train instruction librarians in the practical skills that aren't often taught in library school.

At specific moments during the academic year, it can be helpful to reflect on how your instruction department is weathering academic demands. Even if it is only once a year, departments need some time to perform routine checks and balances on how they are working within the larger system and correct any minor issues that might have arisen in the past. A common technique employed by many libraries is to have an instruction workshop once or twice a year. This workshop is designed to be attended by all staff members who participate in instruction in any meaningful way. It can be as short as an hour or two or as long as a whole-day event. It can be held on campus or, depending on the tone of the meeting, in neutral territory either off campus or in a different campus building. This can often be done as part of a yearly wrap up for all areas of librarianship, so that instruction may be summed up in review for the other areas of librarianship such as collection development and reference that may also need a summative view.

Fundamental Instruction Techniques

Library schools are wonderful places that inspire future librarians about the many varied roles and functions of a librarian and ultimately inspire them to discover the types of professionals they want to become. Classwork explores the depths of what the field can be, and students take the courses that they anticipate they will need in their future work. After librarians have snagged those jobs, however, they are surprised that the workforce varies wildly from the information paradise that most library schools are. The realities of available jobs versus the skills librarians are trained in can lead to librarians who are wonderful and skilled in some areas but perhaps have never actually taught in a classroom setting. Or if they have taught, it has not been in depth or at an advanced level. This is OK. It is what is expected of most new librarians. Keeping this in mind, however, the instruction coordinator faces the challenge of how to introduce a new librarian to instruction while still upholding the rigor and standards that the department is associated with across the university.

The first step for the instruction coordinator is to establish the skill levels of new instructors. If you assume they have no skills or have more than they have from the very start of your relationship, this sets both you and the instructors up for failure. Ideally, you will learn this during the interview process, but even after that, it can be useful to talk about expectations and desires during their first few weeks at the institution.

> **Shadowing:** A new instructor follows a seasoned instructor into the classroom and observes or assists minimally in order to learn teaching methods and the organizational culture regarding instruction.

Shadowing is a very common technique for new instructors to learn how to teach. Literature and pedagogy are great for teaching the background information and theory, but nothing beats on-the-ground experience. Shadowing can take many forms. Some instructors prefer to sit, watch, and take notes without interacting with the classes in any way. Others like to get their feet wet by helping out the primary instructor in small ways, such as by passing out handouts or by helping answer questions during in-class practice. Other methods involve being more of a coteacher with the primary instructor, but this usually happens after the shadower expresses a level of comfort or desire to co-teach. As the coordinator, it's best to feel out how receptive they are to co-teaching versus teaching alone.

> **Coteaching:** Similar to parallel teaching, coteaching is a practice where a class is taught by more than one individual, each qualified to bring different strengths to the lesson.
>
> **Parallel Teaching:** Two instructors jointly plan a lesson, but then split up a class to be taught separately by the individual instructors. These independent sessions then return together to discuss or collaborate on what they worked on apart. This works particularly well with larger class sections.

The benefits of shadowing are not just for new to instruction librarians but also those who may be new to your institution and are learning how instruction varies at your institution compared to their past institution. This is important to remember because instruction is an institution-specific scenario that can follow different models from one place to another. Even when librarians are very seasoned in instruction, if they have switched jobs from one institution to another, it could be in their best interests to sit and watch a few classes at their new institution just to get a greater sense of how things are done. Veteran instructors at your institution may want a refresher as well, just because it is natural to fall into an instruction rut. Each institution has its own style, and just as styles come into vogue and then peter out, what was popular ten years ago may no longer be now. Pay attention as a coordinator as well, this is a dual sided learning opportunity, because just as you may want to see how they teach, you may well learn new tips and tricks from them that you were unaware of. They were hired for a reason after all!

As an instruction coordinator, you can choose to have new instructors follow specific librarians who might have skills in upper-division instruction or scientific instruction, or you might just have new instructors shadow you so that you can give them tailored and specific insights. Sometimes it comes down to timing. If someone is shadowing you, there are a few simple steps you can take to make things easier for him or her. The most important thing you can do is either sit down beforehand or in email notify new instructors of your plans for the class and how you expect them to interact with you and your students during this time. This does not need to be overly formal, but it is nice for those training to know what they are walking into before class starts. Laying out expectations is good on your part, but also listen for feedback. Usually it is beneficial to introduce new instructors to both the classes and the class instructors if they happen to be attending the session. This can be a brief introduction along the lines of "This is John; he's one of our new instructors, and he'll be helping me out today."

Introductions allow everyone to feel a little more comfortable with the process and provide a more seamless integration later down the instruction road. These premeetings can really help ease the situation, as some instructors may be nervous about coming into a class, especially when they are new to the institution and unfamiliar with the way it works. This can also help with other areas of their liaison or research work down the line, in that it gives them networking connections for future opportunities on campus.

A counterpoint to shadowing that is not done nearly as often is **observation.**

> **Observation:** In-class observation of teaching done through formal or informal methods with feedback to the instructor on what was observed.

Although sometimes intimidating to new instructors, it can be helpful to have the instruction coordinator observe silently in the background how a new instructor handles classes. Before you actually mark down time to sit in on classes, be sure to alert and give advance notice to your instructors so that they know what to expect. Indeed, although this is certainly a time to be on the lookout for potential problems, stress that there will not be punitive actions; it is simply a moment to learn. From these observations, you can get a sense of whether an instructor spends too much or too little time on a subject, has problems addressing a class, or has other issues with flow. The presence of an instruction coordinator or any observer will create a different dynamic for an instructor, and this should be taken as a given. Try to be aware of what is caused merely by an awareness of the presence of the observer and what is a consistent habit of the instructor. The differences between observation and shadowing are who is watching the lesson and what the objective is.

Either before or immediately after the instruction session, try to schedule a one-on-one meeting with the observed instructor to go over specific points. Once again, reiterate that this is not a punitive meeting but merely a checkup to see how the instructor is performing. After all, this can be used as a time for the instruction coordinator to learn which scenarios and types of classes a specific instructor excels at.

In addition to shadowing, every experienced instruction coordinator knows that some classes will require more time and effort for prepping than others, and usually you will want a more experienced instructor to teach these classes. It can also be useful to have some classes in your head that you know will be good courses for new instructors. These will either require less prep time or have professors attached to them whom you know will be lenient or willing to experiment and try new things with their classes. Although these classes may not be easier in terms of content, it can be easier for newer instructors to find their footing and learn in a class where the stakes are not as high. Being aware of these issues can help you better understand who to assign for which classes and what they can handle.

> **Shadowing Tip:** If the primary library instructor is all right with the idea beforehand, use the time during shadowing to speak in the back of the classroom to students who may be struggling or have missed a step to help guide them back on track. This is also a great way to engage with students.

As most experienced instructors can tell you, as you lecture in a classroom, student attention spans do not last long. As the instructor, you have a limited time to engage with your students before they become distracted and begin to play with cell phones or simply space out. With few exceptions, this is bound to happen when students are required to be in a space that they do not necessarily want to be in. The frequently referenced time before minds wander is about ten minutes,[1,2] and while this already seems fairly short, in practice it can often be much shorter when you account for other factors going on in the classroom, such as student relationships, the time of the semester, or the time of day. One of the most common ways to surmount this obstacle is to engage in active learning. Sometimes misinterpreted as a way of making your students physically move around the classroom, this learning style can encompass that but more often focuses on giving students discrete activities to do involving problem solving, discussion, and reading and writing. Active learning takes the learner from being a passive participant to one who helps with discovery and understanding themselves. The goal is to get them involved with the process of learning rather than to spend the entire hour lecturing at them. Lecturing has its place, but for a fifty-minute one-shot class, there are usually better alternatives. Instructors who will only see their students once, maybe twice, face an uphill battle to establish authority, engage their listeners, and convey information. With only fifty minutes to impart the tenets of information literacy, if you want to use lecturing as the basis for your class, you will need to make sure that the content is engaging and interesting and will keep a listener's attention. A good gauge is to consider how you would feel while attending that class yourself. Would you be checking your cell phone? What part would bore you? A frequent complaint from librarians is that to do all these things in such a short time span is simply not possible. A well-designed lesson plan can certainly circumvent some of these problems. Training and workshops can help when we become used to working with a certain type of class or a professor and fail to develop lesson plans with as much detail as we may have in the past. This may happen when we choose a lesson plan as the only one that needs to be used for a specific type of class and fail to update it, or we might just assume that a professor we have worked with in the past will always want the same things out of instruction. While this can be a natural instinct to presume, always ask about a class before teaching to get a sense of what the individual class is like and what is expected from instruction. Even if you have worked with a specific professor many times in the past, it is always useful to approach each new class with fresh eyes.

Focus on ways you can immediately engage the student in the learning

process. Lecturing may be a part of the overall lesson, but help your instructors think of ways that they can incorporate meaningful activities into their
lesson plans. Particularly look out for instructors who seem frustrated by
having to teach to certain types of classes or who hesitate to stray from their
methods. Realistically, we will all teach outside our wheelhouses at some
point, and keeping this in mind helps ease the burden. Some instructors only
feel comfortable teaching to upperclassmen, and others only enjoy teaching
to freshmen. Watch for these signals and offer suggestions to employ as they
work with these particular classes. Some active learning methods involve
partnering students so that they must listen and learn from one another as
they work together to find resources. Other methods include giving the students worksheets and a set time limit, with time allotted for discussion and
lecturing on why the activity unfolded as it did. A dearth of active learning
styles can be found in print and online. Try to keep abreast of not only the
new and exciting lessons but also the ones that have stood the test of time
and work consistently. There will always be a sexy new lesson, but in the
rush to try new things, it is important to remember standbys that work. One
option is to keep a prominent list of options available for your instructors to
browse through. Many people use LibGuides as a sourcebook of options for
their team to use as they plan their lesson. LibGuides offer ease of creation
and availability, but for items that need to be quickly accessed, sometimes
websites like this can fall into the trap of being bookmarked and then lost in a
digital milieu of tabs and things we meant to look at later. If you keep the list
in a highly visible place, either within the classroom space itself or within
the offices used by instruction librarians, you can keep people aware of these
options.

Information literacy in most academic institutions tends to follow the
Association of College and Research Libraries (ACRL) Framework for Information Literacy in Higher Education, which provides a highly thoughtful and
structured approach that can help give purpose to your instruction. Although
the framework is new at the time of this writing, having only been adopted
at ALA's Midwinter Meeting in 2016, it was built on the bones of the ACRL
Information Literacy Standards to address flaws in the old standards. Certainly, some institutions have chosen to either reject the framework or wait
a while longer before fully embracing it. With this in mind, be sure to look
through the framework with your instructors and make an informed decision about whether you will be using this as a model for your instruction

decisions. Conscientious decision-making gives your instructors the ability to teach better and work toward a defined goal. Make sure that all the instructors who work with you not only are aware of the framework but also are trying to structure their own lesson plans around the points. Perhaps not everything will be covered in one lesson, but certainly having an objective for what you want your students to be able to do or take away from a lesson can help you think with more clarity about what you need to do in a class. Of course, newer instructors may be less practiced with this, but even seasoned instructors can use some brushing up or reworking of their lesson plans. Although the framework does not have to be prescriptive and many librarians have their own patterns and routines established, consider it a potential source when thinking of ways to give direction to why information literacy is taught as it is. The language of pedagogy can often be academic and hard to grasp for some, and even if they may be practicing it perfectly, putting the practice into words can often leave people confused and frustrated. The instruction coordinator's role can be to translate these concepts for instructors having difficulty understanding what they are being asked to do. In some cases, you might need to portray the concepts through concrete scenarios so that instructors can perceive exactly how to teach the lesson plan, and in others, you might just need to rephrase the concept another way. Pay attention to how instructors react before assuming a concept needs to be presented in another format; the framework itself is ripe for this confusion. Many have suggested that the framework is too broad or not reflective of how they teach, and others have struggled to understand how exactly they need to present it in the classroom.

Another emerging field in information literacy is the concept of **critical information literacy,** or #critlib as those engaged in online conversation have come to discuss it. These sessions tend to be more than one shot focused, and instead are collaborative and embedded with the course instructor to bring about thoughtful exercises for students.

Finding an instructor who is passionate about critical information literacy means you have found someone willing to put the extra legwork into showing students how to be fully informed and engaged in this world. Sometimes this might mean allowing an instructor to work more on class prep than you would normally anticipate or even for their classes to be offered in a nontraditional environment that differs from what you are used to. Experimentation with instruction is a good thing, and although the results are not always uniform or equal, laying this groundwork can lead to amazing things.

Critical Information Literacy: Evaluating not only information but also the systems that information comes from and having an awareness of the forces that may have created it.

Learning New Methods

Just as new instructors need to learn how to work within your instruction environment, seasoned instructors need to stay on top of their own work as well. It can be all too easy within the field of information literacy to get burned out. The job requires that you work with lots of people and put extended energy into helping others, both of which can create frustration when things become routine or when expectations are not met, from either students, professors, or your own plans. Certainly, everyone goes through fallow periods, and as instruction coordinators, we should not force people to constantly learn or change. However, we can check in with our staff throughout the semester and get a sense of how they feel about classes and the way things are going. We can listen, and we can offer advice when asked. At certain points it may be time for the entire instruction team to learn together so that the focus is diverted from any one particular individual and instead focuses on the goals for the department and where things need to be going. Burnout is real, and it can manifest in many ways. As the COVID-19 pandemic taught us all, burnout can happen to anyone, but particularly those who are being asked to do too much with too little reward on many fronts.

Burnout: A mental state in which overwork or stress causes people to disengage from their work or interests.

Applied specifically to library instruction, burnout can be related to the fact that "instruction librarians often have marginal status within the higher education community"[3] and can feel as if the amount of effort they put into their work does not match the respect they get.

Signs of burnout include the following:

- fatigue
- insomnia
- detachment
- pessimism
- poor performance

As the instruction coordinator, your job includes looking out for training opportunities and new instruction methodologies that might help your particular team. It is important to stress here that in the majority of scenarios, these should not be used to fix a wrong or a problem in how instruction is being performed at your institution; they are merely to be viewed as continued education opportunities and things you are all learning in order to consider bringing them into your instruction. Some of these opportunities can be incredibly simple, such as gathering to watch an instruction-focused webinar and then discussing it afterward. When considering webinars that would be useful for the group as a whole, be on the lookout for those either published by specific entities or focused on a set skill. This may involve putting yourself on specific listservs or subscriber lists. Do not give in to the temptation to ignore these sometimes overwhelming emails; rather, dedicate some time each week to finding new opportunities. There may well be no opportunities in one week, but over time, you will find something applicable.

Another option is to assign a reading for the group and have everyone convene the next week to discuss how those methods could be incorporated into their own lesson plans. This can be as simple as having the group read the latest issue of a journal or a chapter of a book. You can also look to other departments and units when considering new techniques. Frequently, we get so locked into our ways and methods that it can act as a refresher to see how others are working. You might take a fieldtrip to another local library or meet with the heads of other departments, such as technical services or circulation, to get a sense of how they manage projects and time. You may already have a sense of this from other library events, but focusing on particulars can highlight things you were unaware of. If you should visit a local library, it can sometimes be overwhelming to see others' instruction spaces. Some think that because a library has better resources or a space with a better instructional design, this specific library is more capable of offering advanced library instruction. It is important to nip these fears in the bud, because while specific circumstances will always vary and some libraries will always have the dream budget, we are all working on the same basic ideas. Instead, when you have all reconvened at your own library, take time to talk with the staff about what excited them about the trip. If necessary, keep a list on a whiteboard or large notepad so that everyone can visualize favorite ideas and tool sets. Divide these into columns such as Good, Bad, Not for Us, or some variant therein. By visualizing these ideas, you can get a clear picture of what your staff wants to focus on. During these times of brainstorming and cooperation, the instruction coordinator should take care to watch how the staff work together. See who is leading the group and who is quietly deferring. Are people working together in harmony, or are they arguing over what they saw? Although there will likely be no need to jump in and deter them one way or the other, you can (1) use these observations to get a feel for how your department is running and (2) use them later when deciding who would be best suited for which classes. From a fiscal perspective and from a new pandemic perspective, we can now use Zoom to go to libraries and locations that might previously have been geographically impossible for an entire team of instruction librarians. Using video conferencing tools like Zoom can help to bring in guest speakers who can take one on one questions from your librarians about the nitty gritty of instruction and how-tos. Think strategically about what type of librarians you've always wished you could talk to, and see if you can't work into your instruction budget an annual honorarium to bring in a guest speaker to help teach and motivate your team.

Once the initial excitement is over, take stock of what stood out and encourage instructors to think of ways that they can incorporate similar methods into their own instruction. Is this something they can do with your student body or something they feel capable of? If they do not feel capable of it at the moment, what do they need in order to? If it is something simple like supplies or equipment, make a note of it and try to find funding. Not infrequently, instruction departments will have a small discretionary budgetary line to spend toward instruction incentives or other small-ticket items that will aid instruction in some manner. For small items, this is fine, but even for larger items, it can be worth it to scout out grants and funding opportunities. This manner of evaluating resources is often good not just for site visits but for any new type of material used by another library. What works for one library simply might not work for yours. It could be a case of personality driving the success of that program, or it could be something harder to recreate at your own library, like a popular group that cannot be re-created. The point is that although you should watch the horizons for new and exciting ways to change things up, do not go in with the assumption that all methods will work immediately.

What's Working

Taking time to reflect on the good parts of your team's instruction is just as important as looking at what is faltering. Such reflection allows you to see where strengths lie and to evaluate what makes them strengths versus other, weaker areas. Perhaps you have an instruction librarian who excels at giving orientations because he or she likes large groups and has a flare for showmanship. However, another librarian in your group might loathe giving orientations yet for some reason—perhaps issues of timing—is the one giving the most orientations. This is a simple issue to fix, as you can rearrange who teaches what. Perhaps you can spend a workshop focusing on what the librarian who does not like giving orientations would prefer to do instead. What is good about these workshops, though, is that by focusing on what is working, you can then figure out what it is about your approach that allows you to be good in those areas and carry that particular strength over into other things. Later in the book we will go over curriculum mapping (see chapter 8) and how that can help direct where particular instructors focus their energy on selecting and choosing classes.

Consider a common scenario in which you are frequently booking instruction sessions with one department—say, communications—and you have, by all accounts, a good relationship with the professors in this field and an understanding of what they need from a typical instruction session. This is a clear strength you can focus on. But what makes this a strength? What is it about your relationship with communications that has allowed the colleagues to work together so well? If you look at it in more depth, you might realize that part of this strength comes from being invited to departmental meetings at the beginning of the year, having an honest dialogue about what you can do for the department, and keeping them in the loop about new changes that might be coming, either new databases or journal subscriptions that are about to be cut and would affect their specific department. However, if you reflect on another department—say, business—you might notice that you have a much weaker relationship with that department. Instruction statistics could show that you teach fewer classes for them and that your instructor evaluations frequently have lower ratings than in any other area. Focus on the difference between these two departments. It could be something simple, or it could be more complex, but by focusing on your strengths with the communications department, you can at least see patterns and methods you can apply to other departments in order to improve both relationships and the classes being taught. For example, maybe library instructors need to start attending department meetings in business at the start of the year. When holding a reflective workshop, sometimes the simplest reason to focus on the strengths is that it is nice to have a balm for your wounds. Not all workshops are happy times. Expect interdepartmental strife and expect people who do not want to spend a whole day talking about their teaching when they could be doing any number of critical tasks; in short, do not expect a perfect workshop. Focusing on the strengths at least allows people to relax a bit, find things they can be proud of, and share how they accomplished these things. Certainly, the whole day should not be seen as one of showering praise, but instead try to think of it as stacking the pain so that you get the hard parts over with first and then can spend the rest of the day working on the things about instruction that everyone actually enjoys. So absolutely focus on why the business department does not reply to your emails and why the athletic orientation went poorly, but mete out this criticism first thing and then find more positive things to focus on. A well-structured day of learning will go quickly regardless, but ending on a negative note casts a dark shadow on the whole day.

An often unspoken element that makes a particular instruction department excel over any other is less the individual activities of team members in terms of their particular instruction strengths and much more how the department relates to one another on a personal level. If people do not feel safe relating to one another, feel no need to share, and are simply put in a toxic situation, all other areas of their work will suffer. By holding workshops, you offer staff a time to not only strengthen their own skills but learn from one another and share about their personal lives. There need not be Kumbaya singing and trust falls, but spending time with our colleagues allows us to get to know one another, and if tensions exist between staff, this could be a good time to work on them. Although not directly instruction related, it is an aspect that reflects on our work as instructors and will eventually pay off. Certainly, greater issues involving harassment and aggression need to be brought to human resources rather than worked out in a workshop, but if it is as simple as new colleagues having joined the team and no one really knowing them yet, this is a perfect time to learn about their backgrounds and what got them involved with instruction.

Workshops are useful tools, but they cannot be applied to all situations without some systematic thought about the content and subject of the workshop.[4] This may sound onerous, but to reiterate an earlier point, would you attend a workshop without knowing what you would get from it? Some topics do not lend themselves to being worked on together through groupthink and discussion, but many topics gain strength through forums like workshops. Running a successful workshop or staff training will require some structure on the part of the instruction coordinator. Think through what you want your staff to walk away from the workshop knowing, and how they will get there. Do they need structured activities? Do they need to read articles in advance of meeting? All of these choices can help guide a successful workshop. In particular, you will need at minimum a defined purpose statement, goals and objectives for the meeting and a way to evaluate whether the workshop was successful.[5] In-person workshops are best for local groups, but if you have a larger group or one spread out over a wider geographical area, you may want to consider using a synchronous video conferencing application such as Google Hangouts, Skype, or Zoom. Although asynchronous video conferencing may be considered for these workshops, the merits of having everyone meet together to work in unison are that they allow for unity and on-the-spot thinking that does not always happen as naturally with asynchronous methods. However, if your group has lots of experience with online course modules, this may be a natural thing to slip into. Particularly for departments that are spread out over many campuses, this can be a real life saver. Follow your gut and work with what you know you and your staff will be comfortable with.

Ongoing Training

Some things simply cannot be learned in their entirety during the course of a workshop. In the case of new software or hardware your university may have implemented, you can use a workshop to begin to learn the fundamentals, but it may be wise to set up a series of training sessions or drop-in days where staff can learn how to use a bit of the software in small chunks. Instruction software in particular tends to make instructors nervous, as they worry about failure during class time. This is a valid concern given how technology can and has affected some notable failures. Although it will be hard to alleviate these fears entirely, as the coordinator, you can create an environment where failure is not a disaster but an acceptable outcome, and you can see to it that everyone has had proper training on a new technology before it is forced onto the instructors. In particular, if only one instructor has a strong desire to use the new technology, by all means, let him or her be the one to run with that and explore it in the classroom. If you sense reticence about the technology from the rest of your instruction team, do not push it. Sometimes it is best to let someone else take the reins and guide others into it when they are ready and have seen the results for themselves. Examples of new technologies like this might include web presentation software like Prezi or software that involves linking up mobile devices via Bluetooth or Wi-Fi. These technologies are simple yet have a high potential for failure because they rely on services that could drop or go out at a crucial moment. Although server issues and tech failures can never completely be prevented, having "what if" plans in place can help ease tensions. Also consider that at some point your team may need to use software to be more inclusive of their students, at which point that goes beyond their personal reticence is a need to make the classroom space equitable for all students. A good example of this might be using an FM system for the hard of hearing or making use of closed captioning in their prepared videos.

It can be easy to forget about conferences as training sources for the group at large, but many librarians go to conferences to further their educations with specific agendas in mind. If your library or department has institutional funds available for travel and professional development, another option is national conferences. Several major national conferences happen annually and biannually. Good instruction coordinators should be on the lookout for instruction-oriented conferences that they can recommend their librarians attend. Keep an eye out for conferences that are both important to attend and cost effective. Know that for some institutions, it may not be financially feasible to go to more than one conference a year, so you must be choosy or try to set a schedule for when to attend which ones. There are several instruction-oriented conferences, but also consider those that may fall outside the library field, as they often have cross-disciplinary sections or talks that may be of use to the librarian. The following are some unranked highlights:

- LOEX (Library Orientation Exchange)
  - If you are involved in any form with instruction, many believe this to be one of the best options for learning about instruction from those who practice and think critically about it.

- Library Instruction West
  - Often confused with LOEX, this standalone conference also deals entirely with instruction, and when factoring in price, it can be a great deal for those librarians based on the West Coast.
- Digital Humanities Summer Institute
  - At first this conference may not seem related to instruction, but it encompasses all aspects of digital humanities work, and instruction librarians looking to bring digital aspects into their instruction could find great pedagogical ideas here.
- Information Literacy Summit
  - Held primarily in the Midwest, this conference is focused on how all branches of education can work together to find ways to support information literacy.
- Computers in Libraries
  - This is another conference that is slightly out of left field when you think of instruction, but as with the Digital Humanities Summer Institute, this is a place to broaden and explore how information literacy is taught, especially if any form of online instruction is offered at your institution.
  - Critical Librarianship & Pedagogy Symposium
      A relatively new conference created by Nicole Pagowsky, this focuses specifically on the critical librarianship and instruction.

While these and other conferences can be great opportunities for learning, networking, and spreading your own ideas, they are expensive and time intensive. One of the harder things to deal with when trying to attend professional development opportunities is that so many of them take place either at the same time of the year (summer) or during peak instruction times like the beginning of the semester, when it can be hard to get away from the library. If cost and time make it hard for the instruction team to wander far from the library, keep in mind local options. Most state library associations hold annual conferences, and although these are frequently public library–oriented, often you can find one or two sessions concerning instruction. In addition to being close, these local conferences tend to be less costly than their national sisters. Aside from local conferences, look for hosted workshops and seminars that may be put on by the state university, your state library, or even the public library. These local workshops and conferences offer a great way to stay involved with the professional landscape without expending a great deal of money, travel time, or work time. Indeed, while national conferences come with all the glamour and excitement of traveling to a new area and meeting with national colleagues, the work produced by local conferences can be just as interesting and offer more relevant information tailored to your specific local population. Many instruction librarians try to moderate their conference attendance to one national conference a year with several smaller conferences intermixed. One benefit to the pandemic was that so many conferences were forced to go virtual, thus lowering the cost and making more accessible training that others would not normally have been able to afford to attend. We shall see in coming years whether this trend continues.

Conferences and workshops are great, but they are not the only option for training. Scholarly communication is beginning to redirect into a variety of different models, including open access publishing and online conferences.[6] In particular, look at other online options such as the following:

- Lynda.com
- T Is for Training
- TechSoup for Libraries
- ALA TechSource

All these online options provide brief topical trainings that can take staff an hour to learn and can be quickly reaccessed and rewatched if you have a staff member who needs more time to study or learn independently. Realistically, the majority of staff training may have to take place locally or online if only because cost can quickly scale up as your staff grows larger. The majority of these resources are free, but some, like Lynda.com, may have small subscription fees and benefit not just staff but students as well. If you are at a larger university, the university may already pay for it through a database subscription. Those of us who are not at a large institution, however, need to be inventive in looking for low-cost and informative training opportunities. Many people are sensitive about learning in groups or would like more time to focus in their own unique ways. Giving them options that allow them to learn at their own pace in a self-directed manner helps alleviate fears and strengthen technological ties at the same time. The best thing you can do as an instruction coordinator is to step back and allow your instructors to show you what they need and move from there without making presumptions about how they need to learn. People learn best when they are learning what they are interested in!

Some training opportunities need not be for direct skills that the instructors themselves will use in their day-to-day jobs but for technologies and skills that your students may request or require as they receive instruction. Particularly, think about this with learning assistive software such as DiLL (Digital Language Lab) for language learning labs, text-to-speech software, recorders, and other software suites. It can be worth partnering with other departments at your institution that may specialize in education technology focused on disability and access.[7] These offices tend to have varied names by institution, but be sure to speak with the leaders of these departments to see if you can incorporate any of their methods into your own instruction. Many techniques require very little extra work on your part and simply require a change in presumptions and class structure that is easy to incorporate into lesson plans.

The online world of social media is usually put down for its fluffy nature, but a wealth of valuable instruction methods can be hidden within. Twitter and blogs have become major sources of inspiration and learning for librarians. They allow for quick updates and a less formalized approach to learning, which models the methods people use in other areas of their lives outside of librarianship. In particular, once you have followed a significant number of librarians on Twitter, you will naturally begin to learn about new and popular conferences that are relevant to your interests if only through back-channeling by way of conference hashtags and discussions.[8] These conversations behind the conversations allow instruction coordinators to get a sense of what is being discussed without actually attending the conference. In the best cases, it allows coordinators to avoid costly fees for a conference if the conversation alludes that it is particularly bad. Lest you think this is only a cost-saving measure, it can also promote conferences you would never have been aware of outside of Twitter. These hashtags can also be used for nonconference events that can be useful in terms of simple awareness of what professionals are discussing at that moment. These trending topics can be double-edged swords in that they allow for an awareness of cutting-edge technology and forefront thinking, but they also create narrow filter bubbles where you only hear one side of the conversation or perhaps see only one aspect of librarianship. One also may fear checking the hashtag after a talk and finding how poorly received the talk was. When setting up an account, try to follow as many different types of accounts as possible. Think of not just who is a librarian but also what type of librarianship is practiced, be it instruction, cataloguing, digital scholarship, and so on and even public libraries versus academic libraries. Each of these can have very distinct types of conversations about their work. By following various types of librarians (and information professionals), you will have access to the multitude of conversations circulating about what is trending in librarianship.

One of the biggest reasons for workshops and ongoing training is that information is not static. We try to stress this to our own students in information literacy lessons. Why would we ignore our own advice? Best practices change, and what worked in the past may no longer be the preferred option. Once again, let me repeat this part, because it is important: Information is not static, and what worked in the past may not always work. Continuous learning is almost a requirement in this field. If you practice what you preach to your own students, your own instruction is likely to be stronger for it, making your words more believable to the students.

Summary

Instruction coordinators need to provide a great deal of training for their instructors, in long-term formats as well as those needed only once a year or so, such as retreats. A particular focus on observation and shadowing can help new instructors learn how to approach pedagogy when they may not have as much classroom time logged as seasoned instructors.

Worksheets and Activities

FIGURE 3.1

Assessing your instruction team's strengths during a workshop

Step 1: Fill out the chart below, asking each instructor to discuss his or her favorite class.

Instructor	Class	What worked	Why?
Common strengths of all:			

Step 2: Look at your common strengths and discuss how these strengths could be duplicated and applied elsewhere.

FIGURE 3.2

Shadowing checklist

Instruction librarian: _____ Class: _____

Shadow librarian: _____ Duration: _____

Step 1: While observing a librarian teaching in a classroom, try to answer as many of these questions as possible. If you don't know how to answer a question, describe it as best you can.

Observations	
What type of pedagogy is the instructor using?	
How do students react?	
How does the instructor use the space?	
Are computer demonstrations easy to follow? Read?	
Are handouts clear and meaningful?	
What type of evaluation is the instructor using to determine the success of the class?	
Anything else?	

Step 2: After the class, sit down with the instructor and instruction coordinator and review and discuss the observations.

Think, Pair, Share Activity

Think, pair, share is a common classroom technique to get students engaged and thinking about concepts in a way that allows for steady engagement on their parts. This activity is great for freshman and entry-level courses where an instruction librarian has sent work ahead for the class before meeting.

This guided method of discovery can let students come to a conclusion on their own rather than having an instructor lecture on it.

Before Class: Send a short article to the professor to distribute, or if embedded with the class, distribute it to students over the course management system with instructions for them to read it prior to the class meeting.

During Class: Break students up into small groups no larger than four students per group. Assign a portion of the article and offer each group a specific question related to the section.

Give students at least ten minutes (if not more, depending on the duration of individual classes) to discuss their takes on the reading as well as their particular responses to that question.

After the ten minutes have elapsed, have each group report on their question and the response they came up with as a group. With coaching, this will become a whole-class discussion.

Example prompt questions (to be modified relating to your specific article/assignment):

1. What context is the author writing this from?
2. What are the barriers a student would face in participating in this conversation?
3. What methods would be needed to recreate this experiment?

NOTES

1. Karen Wilson and James H. Korn, "Attention during Lectures: Beyond Ten Minutes," *Teaching of Psychology* 34, no. 2 (2007): 85–89.
2. Wilbert James McKeachie and Graham Gibbs, *McKeachie's Teaching Tips: Strategies, Research, and Theory for College and University Teachers* (Boston: Houghton Mifflin, 1999).
3. Maria Accardi, "What Is Burnout?," accessed July 5, 2017, https://librarianburnout.com/2015/03/.

4. Jennifer Koerber, "Manage the Device Deluge," *Library Journal* 140, no. 9 (2015): 28–31.
5. S. Gerding, "Transforming Public Library Patron Technology Training," *Library Technology Reports* 47, no. 6 (2011): 43–51.
6. Justin Shanks and Kenning Arlitsch, "Making Sense of Researcher Services," *Journal of Library Administration* 56, no. 3 (2016): 295–316.
7. Margaret E. S. Forrest, "Disability Awareness Training for Library Staff: Evaluating an Online Module," *Library Review* 56, no. 8 (2007): 707–15.
8. H. Fiester and T. Green, "Student Use of Backchannels," *TechTrends* 60, no. 4 (2016): 404–8.

FURTHER READINGS

Accardi, Maria. "What Is Burnout?" Accessed July 5, 2017. https://librarianburnout.com/2015/03/.

Critten, J. "Ideology and Critical Self-Reflection in Information Literacy Instruction." *Communications in Information Literacy* 9, no. 2 (2015): 145–56.

Fiester, H., and Green, T. "Student Use of Backchannels." *TechTrends* 60, no. 4 (2016): 404–8.

Gerding, S. "Transforming Public Library Patron Technology Training." *Library Technology Reports* 47, no. 6 (2011): 43–51.

Koerber, Jennifer. "Manage the Device Deluge." *Library Journal* 140, no. 9 (2015): 28–31.

Forrest, Margaret E. S. "Disability Awareness Training for Library Staff: Evaluating an Online Module." *Library Review* 56, no. 8 (2007): 707–15.

McKeachie, Wilbert James, and Graham Gibbs. *McKeachie's Teaching Tips: Strategies, Research, and Theory for College and University Teachers.* Boston: Houghton Mifflin, 1999.

Shanks, Justin, and Kenning Arlitsch. "Making Sense of Researcher Services." *Journal of Library Administration* 56, no. 3 (2016): 295–316.

Stephens, Michael. "Exemplary Practice for Learning 2.0." *Reference and User Services Quarterly* 53, no. 2 (2013): 129–39.

Wilson, Karen, and James H. Korn. "Attention during Lectures: Beyond Ten Minutes." *Teaching of Psychology* 34, no. 2 (2007): 85–89.

Management

Introduction

Many librarians don't think directly about leadership and management when they get into the field, which is a shame, because there are so many amazing opportunities for great leaders within. Since the position of instruction coordinator can vary so wildly from institution to institution, your particular role may or may not have supervisory skills associated with it. This chapter focuses on how to arrange and schedule classes that may have varied needs and time demands as well as how to manage the people you work with. For further information, consider the former ALA division LLAMA (Library Leadership and Management

Association) now CORE: Leadership, Infrastructure, Futures for training and ideas and as a general sounding board when you run up against a particular frustration that they may be able to help with. Management within libraries encompasses a wide range of needs, techniques, and areas. In this specific chapter, we are looking at management from the viewpoint of how an instruction coordinator can help manage not only their instruction librarians but also expectations and time surrounding classroom scheduling and working with faculty outside the library. Scheduling can quickly become a nightmare when space is limited for the instruction itself, and some needs have to be prioritized while others take a backseat. Knowing how to set clear expectations and boundaries will at least help others understand why things are done the way they are. Managing expectations is half the battle.

In librarianship, there is often a perceived need to foresee what troubles may be around the next corner. This need has often been focused on understanding new technologies and the ways we can access them and aid our students. While this is an admirable worldview, others such as Woodard and Hinchcliffe have pointed out that this fear cannot be adequately put at the feet of one particular monster; instead, the confluence of many challenges at once—such as new technologies, changing access methods, and enhanced learning methods—troubles us the most.[1] Use this chapter as a way not to focus on one particular worry but to form a cohesive thought process on how to deal with varying forms of management. Just as we build so much of our pedagogical practices around the framework of information literacy, similar ideas can be applied to the unique situation of managing librarians and the information systems we watch over. A great deal of the day-to-day job will involve some level of management, and as you become more familiar with the role, it will become closer to second nature to apply some of the techniques highlighted in this chapter.

Scheduling

When planning who will teach what and when, especially with a larger staff of instruction librarians, things will quickly become confusing if the instruction program does not have a system or plan in place for how to deal with instruction requests or even the simple task of booking space. In the opposite situation of a library with a smaller staff, perhaps with only one or two other instruction librarians working with the instruction coordinator, scheduling can become an issue of trying to meet demand. Like many things in the academic world, information literacy has a season, and during that season, instruction librarians will find themselves booked completely and busy beyond belief. Not only are they scheduling multiple classes and hoping that they can find some time to work on their own projects, but multiple instruction librarians are competing to find the time and space to teach classes during the same times. Some libraries are blessed with multiple instruction spaces, and others are blessed just to have a dedicated space for instruction.

The physical realities of instruction are often some of the largest barriers to successful information literacy instruction. The lesson plans may be carefully laid out, but if there is no space to teach them, there is no chance for the lesson to even get off the ground. Likewise, sometimes spaces might not be available with adequate technology for the lesson plan. Sometimes the Wi-Fi is unreliable in a space where you were hoping to have students access resources with laptops; other times, a classroom may have no computers at all, or the podium and seating may be structured so that students cannot pair off into groups and the instructor cannot easily walk among the groups. Physical considerations such as these will have major ramifications for how a lesson plan is actually delivered. It is the instruction coordinator's responsibility to keep in mind instructors' tendencies when trying to find appropriate spaces. Being aware of the fact that a particular class will be using computers heavily helps you schedule it in a location with an adequate amount of computers. At the very least, it allows you to forewarn instructors of the limitations of certain spaces in advance so that they can tailor their lesson plans to match the space. One of the duties of an instruction coordinator is to ensure that the instructors they supervise do not walk blindly into a classroom without being aware of what to expect from the physical space. Physical realities may seem superficial, but they are often the first stumbling blocks. Tangible realities need to be addressed when considering instruction. Items being too high for the average instructor to reach or seats being uncomfortable to sit in for long periods of time will affect how instruction is performed and received.

Class Outside the Library: An Example

A librarian is assigned to teach to a sophomore-level history class, but there is no space in the library for the class. She agrees to meet the class in their regular classroom. Before developing a lesson plan, she goes to the room after hours and sees that the only equipment available is a projector and a computer with HDMI hookups for laptops. Unfortunately, the computer is not set up for her user account. She needs the class professor to log her in. She also sees that the student desks are modular and can be arranged into interlocking groups. Now she knows to arrive early, to ask students to bring their laptops, and that she can design a group work activity.

Another consideration to be aware of when thinking about the creation of a library specific classroom is that many people feel that they need to guard against their space being taken over by nonlibrary instruction. As one librarian put it, "If bookings by teaching faculty were allowed, the Lab would not be available for library instruction sessions."[2] Not all libraries have a policy that teaching faculty are not allowed to teach in library spaces, but as the instruction coordinator, put careful thought into your rationalization for why teaching faculty will or will not be allowed to use the space so that when requests come your way, you have a policy to point to and a way to respond to dissatisfaction. Scheduling with these competing demands requires the instruction coordinator to balance the needs of many and figure out a method that will accommodate all their specific institutional needs. Critically, with so many demands on their time, many instruction coordinators report that at the end of the day, they just want to make sure that requests are met and classes are taught.

There are three main types of scheduling to be aware of as you begin to choose the method that is right for your institution: flexible scheduling, fixed scheduling, and mixed scheduling.[3] Of the three types of scheduling, perhaps the most common to instruction librarians is flexible scheduling, which requires instruction to occur at the request of a student or professor as opposed to being held at a fixed time.[4] For the majority of librarians, a typical scenario is for a subject professor to contact the instruction coordinator to arrange a time for his or her class to meet with a librarian. At the end of the chapter, you will find a worksheet that focuses on the key information the instruction coordinator needs to take away from that conversation and convey to the librarian who will eventually teach that class or series of

classes. One of the most common points of failure with instruction scheduling is a lack of communication between the professor and the librarian. If
they have differing expectations about what will happen in the class or who
is showing up, then dissatisfaction occurs. As the instruction coordinator, it
is your job to consider what you have learned from the professor and choose
an appropriate instructor. From there, the librarian teaching the class will
need to contact the professor and discuss the details of what will happen in
the class. This situation can work extremely well in a small institution, but
in a larger institution that teaches multiple classes at the same time, other
methods may need to be employed. You could base class assignments solely
on subject area, knowing that certain instructors will only teach to art majors
or music majors. Likewise, you could defer class scheduling to individuals
so that it is on the librarians to arrange and schedule classes on their own,
making sure that they keep you in the loop on what classes are being taught
and to whom. Some instruction coordinators found it so deeply frustrating
to rely on teaching faculty to provide all the necessary information (course
numbers, students, dates and times, types of content desired) that instead of
having professors make requests via email or phone, they switched over to an
online form with all the necessary information on it. The professor then fills
out this form and the instruction coordinator follows up after processing the
information.[5] While it may be tempting to flip the model so that the onus falls
on the teaching faculty, this method still requires the instruction coordinator
to follow up and make sure that what the teaching faculty requested is what
they actually meant or check why they did not mention certain aspects.

When more than one classroom is involved, scheduling allows you to
know who is in what room at what time so that there are no overlaps or
conflicts. Likewise, just as instructors vary in skillsets, rooms vary in technological abilities and scale. You may have a small classroom that can only
seat twenty students, and you may have a large classroom that can seat up
to sixty students. Knowing where to book a class is dependent on knowing
what students will get out of each instruction space. Capacity is one obvious issue, but another issue to be aware of is technological needs, such as
whether particular software suites are installed on the computers or even *if*
computers are available for use. Increasingly, there has been a trend toward
creating classrooms without desktop monitors, instead relying either on **cows**
with laptops charged and waiting or moveable furniture so that the space can
be used in multiple ways. Such spaces can adapt to group work and accommodate students with disabilities.

What's a cow? A storage locker for laptops, this is a loving acronym for "computers on wheels." The lockers can come in a variety of formats and include the potential to charge laptops when not in use.

In an age of multimodal instruction, having a room that can be used in multiple ways is a bonus, but when scheduling it, you need to be aware of the needs of a class and the classroom's ability to accommodate those needs. For instance, some professors are just happy that you came to their classes, offered their students worksheets, and gave a brief lecture about what they can do at the library (use the writing center, check out laptops, etc.) and don't care whether you provide a full-fledged demonstration of specific tools. Particularly in the case of large groups, where the class size is larger than normal, rather than thinking in an all-or-nothing manner, speak with the professor to see if the class can be split up, with half (or even a third) of the students coming in on one day and the other students coming in on another day. If you have multiple instructors at your disposal, consider having the class come in at the same time but with two librarians teaching the same lesson plan in two different spaces. This is a great solution when a professor insists that the instruction cannot take place over more than one day, perhaps accounting for a very rigid syllabus. To do so requires multiple instructors and a pared-down lesson plan, but it is possible.

Campus Mapping

During high-use times, it pays to know of places on campus outside the library that you can use for instruction. Walk through your academic buildings looking for computer labs and reservable spaces where you could imagine teaching a library class. Think about all types of instruction, and resist the temptation to think of just the standard types, particularly with large classes and those that are not demonstration oriented. Take notes on potential locations and write down contact information to request to use them.

Institutions have adopted various models to manage different spaces, instructors, and classrooms. The number-one thing you will need is a calendar system. At this point, very few instruction programs are using a paper system, but you could be using Microsoft Outlook, Google Calendars, LibCal or YouCanBook.me.[6] Even scheduling software such as WhenToWork could be useful if you have student workers involved with the instruction process in some way. Many types of open source scheduling software have appeared on the market in recent years, and each has its pros and cons. When looking for scheduling software, ease of use and ability for multiple people to have access are key. Doodle polls can also be useful for scheduling meetings but would not be practical for most instruction scenarios given that most professors have class at a fixed time and cannot have students come in at any other time. The same applies to respecting students' schedules. They work and take other classes. Their schedules are not as flexible as some would imagine, and they cannot always just drop into the library. Another important point is that Doodle works best with more than two parties. Two people can easily talk or email about their schedules, but when more than two people are in the mix, Doodle shines. However, rarely is more than one person involved in arranging a time and place to meet when scheduling a class. Springshare has LibCal, a calendar application that can be used in many different ways. Many libraries are already familiar with Springshare's most notable product, LibGuides. Libraries such as California State University, Dominguez Hills, have begun to use LibCal to allow professors to arrange their own instruction sessions without the need to contact a specific librarian. Rather than librarians having to negotiate with professors who are blind to what is available in terms of classroom space and timing, they can now see what times and spaces are available for themselves. When you implement new technologies and software, you will run into differences from your prior method, so be aware of what these differences are as you weigh the pros and cons of each method. While you work on finding a way to effectively schedule, remember that you are not locked into one particular model once you try it. Certainly, some services have fees, and you may not want to lose out on that cost, but if a service or model of scheduling is not working, feel free to try something else. It's better to try multiple options than stick with one thing that only partially meets your needs. We are in a golden age of instructional technology; it pays to find the method that works for you and your institution, even if that means trying multiple options. The biggest issue when testing out new options is making sure that, from the end-user perspective, your students and subject professors see little to no change or have few issues with the process.

Scheduling instruction often rests on the paradigm of a subject professor contacting the library, usually by either email or phone, and requesting instruction for a specific time and date, and then the library responds by saying whether or not they can teach the class. This has worked well in the sense that a need is being met, but it ignores a large portion of professors who may not think to contact the library or who may not be aware of the need for information literacy instruction. This allows you to passively run a program, but sitting back and waiting for people to know they need information literacy instruction ignores those who would be interested but are unaware of the program. In many ways, the instruction coordinator needs to act as an ambassador for the program and find ways to get the attention of these subject professors in ways beyond the tradition of the professor contacting the library. Consider cribbing notes from the outreach librarians you may know. You might simply go where the subject professors will be and talk to them. If you rely on people to contact you based on a pamphlet they may have been given when they were first hired or based on word of mouth from a colleague, the effectiveness will decrease with time. Such grassroots campaigns have worked famously in many different types of marketing, but once a program is established, the instruction coordinator will need to find a more complex way of campaigning besides relying on goodwill and word of mouth. Advocacy is our strongest technique for getting beyond the library walls. Find the people who set the agendas and motives for an institution and make sure that your message is not only honed but understandable to outsiders. Find the natural partners for library instruction and see how they can help encourage people to come into the library. This is the time for your instruction elevator pitch. Show those people what the librarians do, and make sure they know why your work is important.

In most forms of scheduling, consistency is a strong goal to aim for.[7] As has been mentioned, though, in the case of library instruction, scheduling can often be built around relationships and a perception of need rather than a predictable pattern. Most instruction coordinators can rely on certain classes being taught each year at roughly the same times with similar information literacy needs. These are often standard 101 courses that a majority of freshmen will take. In some cases, the particular professors may change, but the department will have a recommended syllabus that includes a library visit, so the class remains the same even though professors may cycle in and out. Likewise, many instruction librarians develop preferences for the classes they want to teach and become close with certain subject professors. This is another way to introduce consistency. If you know, for example, that certain professors always want to have specific librarians teach for them, try to reach them before the semester starts so that plans can be set early on and you have a standing appointment.

> **Real Talk:** Many entry-level courses that require information literacy classes are taught by adjuncts. Try to maintain close contact with adjuncts at your university. Frequently, they teach at multiple campuses with a teaching load that leaves little time for extraneous meetings. They may not always be on the same listservs or at the same meetings that you attend at the start of the year, so try to find ways to contact them and plan around their schedules.

Time

Tempus fugit—especially in an academic environment, where you can easily look up from your desk and find that the semester has flown by and you haven't achieved half your goals. Keeping this in mind, it is vital to pay attention to when things are scheduled. The longer you are in the role of instruction coordinator, the more you will come to learn and know the fluctuations of your institution. As you get busy, you must learn to stress the value of your own time and the value of the time of your librarians. This includes both an awareness of how much prep goes into lesson planning and long-term planning and also a realization that in a highly social field, some relationships in academia take time to flourish. A common issue with instruction scheduling is for professors to call up the library the day or week before class and ask to have library sessions taught for them with no advance warning. It will be up to you to set a policy regarding this situation, so consider the following:

- Regardless of whether there is space in the calendar, a lesson plan cannot be adequately made and prepared with a day's notice.
- Without planning in advance, your time and lessons have been undervalued as not worthy of advanced notice.
- Giving in to such requests establishes an always-ready model, in which your work is expected to be available on demand without your input or control.

While professors might ask for instruction sessions the day before class for very valid reasons and they may well be very nice people, it is all right to establish a boundary for yourself and your librarians. Set a guideline for how much time you and your librarians need to prepare for a class, and stand by it. Yes, this means you may have to turn down some classes. In an assessment-driven institution that loves higher numbers, this can be difficult. A good instruction program runs on quality not quantity, but it is hard saying no to people you respect and admire. Sometimes it is just hard to say no when you look at your calendar and know the class could easily be taught by either you or one of the other instruction librarians. In return for saying no, though, the instruction librarians who work for you will respect that you respected their time by not asking them to make a commitment when they may already be overscheduled. These are, of course, high-minded ideals that in the real world are often met with pleading and convincing arguments for why these classes should be taught. One tactic is to consider asking the content professor, "In an ideal scenario, what will your students gain from this instruction with so little time for my instructors to prepare?" Without any preparation, a class will be more likely to falter and have a weak connection for students. Be careful with this tactic, however. In some cases, it can invite debate, and what you truly want to present in this scenario is a flat no. A response that communicates that there will be no ground to be gained most effectively shutters the door. I highly urge you to stand firm in denying fast turnarounds for instruction. Often the best way to deal with this situation is to offer another time when you can teach and to walk through in your rejection the work you would need to do in the intervening time. These quickly assigned classes do not give anyone a great library experience and are frequently a cover for class babysitting, which is not productive territory for anyone.

Another important time-related detail in coordination is learning the duration of the class and in particular how much time has been allotted for instruction. In some instances, a professor requests instruction but spends so much time going over returned homework, giving instructions for the next class, and providing feedback during the actual class period that the librarian instructor has, in reality, far less time than he or she was accounting for. Much as you may want to, you cannot ask professors, "How much of my time will you waste?" However, you can arrange a realistic schedule, making them aware of how much time you need and seeing where that falls within their own plans. Or while listening to a professor, you might realize that what they want can be more practically and effectively taught during a fifty- or seventy-minute class. This is an excellent opportunity to bring up the concept of embedding or expanding the library session into a multiday lesson. Many professors are initially hesitant to devote so much of their class time to one library-led activity. If you strongly feel that what they are looking for will take up too much time, though, think of ways to develop activities, papers, or lessons that would be valuable to them. Usually this work is established before the start of the semester. In some cases, it may involve a multiphased approach. Perhaps that semester the professor can truly only allot one day of class to the library; in that case, you might mention to him or her that you or another librarian would be willing to collaborate on a lesson plan built into the syllabus that would embrace the elements he or she wants students to learn and get them in the library more than once. Such embedded classes can be some of the most rewarding classes a librarian will teach.

From past roles, you might have experience with scheduling coverage on a reference or circulation desk. A common method of scheduling these locations is to look at how many hours need to be covered and how many hours each particular worker can fill within those set times. A similar method is to take a deep look at the course schedules for your institution and figure out not only when classes are offered but what your staff hours are like. Do you have librarians who are willing to come in after standard work hours to teach to a night class? What about a weekend-only session? These areas can be overlooked when planning a class. In the moment, it is easy to say that you can get someone to teach a 7 p.m. class on a Thursday. In reality, people have lives and plans that may already have been made. Consider especially that some librarians may have to find babysitters or make other arrangements beyond simply showing up to teach.

Depending on whether the instruction session is going to be held in the library classroom space or within another instruction space on campus, locating specific areas can be a major and often forgotten factor in timing. Are there signs in the library directing students and professors to the classroom? Is the classroom clearly marked for people to see?[8] Frequently, instruction coordinators have little control over the look and placement of their specific classroom space, but often they have either the cachet or ability to get better signs and notifications. Keep in mind that although librarians work in the library every day and are deeply familiar with the layout of the building, students—especially freshmen, who may not have been in the library before—are not. Many students are merely told to meet the professor at the library classroom without being given any specifics. Most students can get to the library, as they will have seen it on tours and perhaps done some orientation activities there, but the inside of the building can be overwhelming. If the library is at a large state institution or just particularly large and well-funded, these academic libraries can often appear vastly different from the public libraries students may have grown up with, and they have departments they may never have heard of, such as interlibrary loan or special collections, among others. How do you direct students who may be dealing with such intimidation? With this in mind, it is vital that the reference and circulation desks have access to some form of the instruction calendar. They may not need to see all the specifics of the lesson plans and notes on how the class was formed, but the frontline workers will get questions about where the library classroom is, and it is far better to give them some form of access to allow them to know that there is in fact a class about to happen, and yes, even provide directional support. It is up to the instruction coordinator to decide how to present this calendar to the various desks. It could be in a paper format, but bear in mind that this will have to be updated weekly and sometimes even within the week depending on cancellations and new additions to the roster. Using a shared calendar can often solve the problem of having to keep everyone updated, but it can sometimes create a nest of permissions problems. Very likely, some of the people staffing the reference desk will also be instruction librarians of some flavor, but not necessarily all of them. If you want certain information to stay private, there are two approaches to take with shared calendars. Either be very cautious, aware, and controlling of what information is put into the calendar or try to find a way to monitor just what the permissions you have given mean. They may be classic permissions like read, write, execute, and delete, but there can be a whole host of variables. For example, you may have given someone permission to edit entries, yet they are not actually able to add instructors or spaces. Some instruction coordinators have reported how frustrating managing these permissions can be.

As much as you hope that students will approach the reference desk and ask for directional help, some are shy or anxiety prone about new situations, and in that case, good signage can help. Signs can easily be overlooked or ignored, and even if the student does pay attention to the sign, sometimes the wording is unclear, so the words on the sign itself need to be carefully thought out, striking the right balance between information and clarity. Many literacies are now beginning to be acknowledged, and visual literacy is one of them. If any librarians within your institution have a background in graphic design or visual literacy, get their thoughts on how to redesign or create brand-new library signage. In some cases, this can be done very cheaply, and in others, it may take some money to rebrand the signs across the whole library. It depends on both institutional support and staff motivation. Frequently, the role of an instruction coordinator involves a good deal of being an intermediary and going to find the people who can make it right.

Another aspect of factoring in time to find the classroom falls on the shoulders of the instruction librarians. Not all classes are taught within the library space, and they can frequently be held where the class usually meets or even in a computer lab outside the library. On smaller campuses, locating a specific room may be less of a concern to someone who has worked there a long time, but at a larger institution, not only do you need to know what building the room in, but you need to factor in travel time, perhaps to even drive over there. Just as most people hate to have students arrive late to class and interrupt their lesson, it is equally rude to arrive late to a class that you have been invited to. In an immediate sense, this relays to the professor and the students that you do not perceive them or information literacy as important. The effects of lateness may not be felt until the next semester or next time the class is offered; the professor may choose not to work with that instructor again, or he or she may choose not to work with the library at all. Small slights can carry far. Indeed, when we arrive on time and prepared to present, we show that we respect the time of everyone in that room. Students both traditional and nontraditional are increasingly living in a world that differs from what some of us may imagine when we think of a typical college experience. Many have other things placing demands on their time, from intensive class extracurriculars to full-time jobs, families, and exercise. Honor their time, even if only because they made time to listen to you. And make sure you have something worth saying!

Thinking about classroom space means intentionally thinking about how our physical surroundings affect our teaching performance. Often we believe that we can be dropped into any room and perform the same lesson plan without a perceived influence. Yet many instructors report feeling flustered after arriving in a new or different environment. If you have the option to help be a part of the decision-making process when new classroom spaces are built or updated, try to think intentionally about how the space is used versus what is merely flashy or glamorous. Do people wish for more outlets or for chairs that can move about more easily? These little details add up and can drastically affect how a class functions.

People

One of the distinct problems instruction coordinators face with their role is that very frequently, they are looking after and assigning projects to a crew of people, but they may very well lack supervisory power over them. Some instruction coordinators have supervision built into their job descriptions, but many have job descriptions that cover a wide array of job duties with little to offset that. Increasingly, the instruction coordinator wears many hats beyond just instruction.

So how can you show authority when in practice you may have very little authority? If you are lucky, you have a personality that naturally exudes authority and leadership. If not, what then? The vast majority of library literature on leadership focuses primarily on those in administrative roles, such as a director or a dean, but shockingly little is written for those who have smaller roles that still require a form of leadership. Literature written about library managers, specifically those who work within the academic environment, often pulls from other fields with masters-level terminal degrees, like social work and masters of fine arts. The primary suggestion is that at times, leadership skills can be more accidental than intentional—a happy mix of mentorship, fit, and networking.[9] Robert P. Holley has focused his research on why so many librarians shy away from leadership roles and management in particular. He reflects on what courses are offered to library and information science (LIS) students and, in particular, whether they are required.[10] What is written tends to be focused on which soft skills from each department can translate into leadership skills at the higher administrative level.[11] Bearing these limitations in mind, it can be useful to dip into the larger world of management literature and see how generalized concepts can be applied to libraries, knowing full well that there may be gaps in how things are produced. Just because your title and responsibilities may not reflect leadership, this does not mean that your role cannot have leadership aspects. Taking on the ideal of responsive leadership will give you the bearings to react and adapt your management style to whatever issues may arise.

One guideline that new instruction coordinators can look to is the ALA Standards for *Proficiencies for Instruction Librarians and Coordinators*.[12] This work not only provides clear guidelines on what is expected of instruction coordinators; it also gives clues about how to manage and listen to staff when you are unfamiliar with the specific process. Many instruction coordinators may initially feel like they lack the specific skills to fulfill the role. If they have a guideline like the standards to review, they may see that they are already performing many of the necessary actions. Keeping this in mind, the first step is to start reading and learning about what you do not know. Another step is to be clear, concise, and precise with your words. Naturally, this may seem like a daunting task, especially when you work with people on a day-to-day basis, and at times you will just want to relax. That is to be expected, but when speaking from a managerial role, you must use your words wisely. Take notes frequently, and always put agreements and understandings in writing. Although this may not keep things from going badly in other areas, following up through either email or another written form allows both instruction coordinators and librarians to have clear expectations.[13] Think of this as an insurance policy for both you and the other librarians. Managing expectations is sometimes just the ability to let others know what you can and cannot do and what you will try to accomplish, and even if you eventually fall short of your goals, everyone will know you have tried.

Responsibility to those you are serving means being aware of how you can help others while maintaining and establishing each individual's boundaries. Many people are intimidated by those in positions above them and can react in a variety of ways. However, keep in mind that those in leadership roles, including instruction coordinators, are all seeking to fulfill a goal. When they ask for something like a number, quote, or rationale, they are not looking to exert power and dominance in most cases. They are looking for more information to inform their decision-making processes and ways to meet their goals. Keeping this in mind, interactions should be fairly straightforward. Both parties have the same goals and expectations (hopefully), and each has different skills that can help meet these goals. Win-win, right? Well, mostly. In a perfect world, things move smoothly. In a realistic world, setting up clear expectations and a plan for how to meet them will help make things work a little better. This is why things like learning objectives and needs assessment can be so vital to the instruction coordinator in terms of knowing what to build from. Quality data can help inform decision-making for every person involved. Gallup looked at how managers can encourage engagement specifically by looking at three common attitudes of managers: those who focused on employees' strengths, those who focused on weaknesses, and those who did not focus on either.[14] While employee engagement was strongest with those managers who focused on positive strengths and qualities, the real takeaway was that any engagement is better than none. Employees lose engagement when they lack a sense of purpose or an understanding of their role within the organization. Instruction coordinators should reflect on how their own practices look in relation to their staff. Do your librarians understand the framework? Do they know why they are being asked to perform instruction in a certain way? Giving a purpose to our instructional practices beyond the simple answers can help librarians work harder toward accomplishing those goals. At times your purpose will not align completely with those of the other librarians, but when goals are intentionally created together based on ideas that everyone on the team would like to strive toward, there will be less push back.

A system of shared decision-making, consistent meetings, and clear communication allows everyone to feel happy and confident in the decisions that come from these meetings.[15] Assessment data should not be gathered without purpose. Use the information to help inform the decisions you and your team will need to make about instruction. Underrepresented areas may reveal the need for more instruction, just as sometimes assessment reveals that the work has been so focused on one area that it has become redundant or needs to be tweaked in order to become relevant once more.

Librarians come from diverse backgrounds, and not everyone will respond in the same way, so it behooves the instruction coordinator to develop a general cultural awareness and an openness to learning about other cultures. On a micro level, you may not be able to directly increase diversity, but you can make the atmosphere a little more welcoming so people can feel comfortable expressing their ideas and vocalizing what they need from their work environment. Try not to make assumptions; the old adage about assumptions holds true in that by assuming we know about people's lives and backgrounds, we block them from telling us their own truths and sometimes even prevents staff members from feeling like valued members of the team. Sara Ahmed's[16] work on institutional diversity is particularly illuminating for those who may be new to this field and want to know a little more about how to work with others who come from differing backgrounds. Our students are also included in this work, and it is important to think about how our lessons affect those who may not learn or see the world in the same way we do. We teach to a wide variety of students from extremely varied backgrounds and experiences. Encourage instruction librarians to build their lesson plans around unique learning styles and pedagogies. When trying to find guides to management, look at journals like the *Journal of Library Administration,* which consistently publishes issues facing library managers.

Part of the role of an instruction coordinator is to keep up to date with both the field of instruction, but also the tangential worlds of libraries and look for the ways in which they collide with instruction. Instruction doesn't happen in a silo, and the more inclusive we make it the better it becomes.

Focus on what you know. You know the instruction librarians who work for and with you. Try to understand where they're coming from. For many of us, information literacy is one of the major functions of our jobs, and while we may love all that it represents, it is not all that we are. Learning who performs instruction at your library can inform decisions based on how they approach problems, teaching, and learning. Part of managing is understanding how the social system within a specific organization works[17] and recognizing that certain actions will work with some groups but not others, and this might be based purely on how the institution has historically worked. It may take time for people to retire and new people to be hired. Serving on a

FIGURE 4.1

Scheduling a class

1. How many students are in the class?
2. How much time is allotted for this class?
3. How much time do you need before and after the instruction?
4. What are your goals for this class?
5. Is there anything you would like students to learn specifically in this class?
6. What (information literacy) level are most of the students at?
7. Do you have a librarian preference?

Class duration	Teacher	Room/space
9 a.m.–10 a.m.		
10:30 a.m.–11:30 a.m.		
11 a.m.–12 p.m.		

search committee can help you determine who enters the library as faculty or staff, but by no means does it fully control the final decision. Likewise, rather than simply waiting for the perfect staff, use that time instead to make the staff you have work well. They all have passions, interests, and reasons why they got into this profession. Find ways to tap that latent desire or work around the problems that arise. Waiting is often a form of ignoring an issue, and ignoring solves nothing.

Conclusion

Pick a management style and try your best to be consistent with it. There may be times when it behooves you to reevaluate the process and find another strategy, perhaps based on new colleagues who may have their own methodologies. The number-one thing to keep in mind is that just because something has always been done a certain way, that does not mean that there are no other and better ways. If an instruction coordinator is in a role that does not allow for direct supervision of instruction librarians, that does not excuse that coordinator from needing to be a good manager; it simply means that more thought needs to be put into how ideas and requests are put forward to peers.

Scheduling is quickly transitioning away from a paper-based method, and while several services are on the frontiers for how to manage who teaches what and when, make sure you think about who has access to the information before you commit to one service over another. Also remember that there is no perfect solution for most scheduling issues. There will be classes that no one wants to teach, just as there will be classes that everyone wants to teach. It is the job of the instruction coordinator to find people willing to take on the work, find the right fit, and sometimes just make sure that information literacy is being taught.

Summary

Managing a team of other librarians can create conflict and stress, especially given that many instruction coordinators are not the direct supervisors of the teams they work with. Methods of managing stress and conflict can help ensure that instruction coordinators work well with each group they routinely engage with. Scheduling spaces and shifting technologies will be at the forefront of your day-to-day work, and it will take practice to find the best methods.

NOTES

1. Beth S. Woodard and Lisa Janicke Hinchliffe, "Technology and Innovation in Library Instruction Management," *Journal of Library Administration* 36, no. 1/2 (2002): 39–55.
2. Robert J. Lackie and Edward M. Corrado, "The Multi-purpose Library Computer Lab: Tips and Techniques for Successful Operation and Management," *College and Undergraduate Libraries* 8, no. 2 (2001): 43.
3. Christine A. Hurley, "Fixed vs. Flexible Scheduling in School Library Media Centers: A Continuing Debate," *Library Media Connection* 23, no. 3 (2004): 36–41.
4. Joy McGregor, "Flexible Scheduling: Implementing an Innovation," *School Library Media Research* 9 (2006).
5. Laura A. Staley, "Using Survey Sites for Information Literacy Scheduling and Teaching," *College and Undergraduate Libraries* 14, no. 3 (2007): 103–6.
6. Amanda Nichols Hess, "Scheduling Research Consultations with YouCanBook.me," *College and Research Libraries News* 75, no. 9 (October 2014): 510–13.
7. Roger Stelk and Suping Lu, "Eight Days a Week: The Art of Reference Desk Scheduling," *Reference Librarian* 28, no. 59 (October 1997): 37.
8. Mark Aaron Polger and Amy F. Stempler, "Out with the Old, in with the New: Best Practices for Replacing Library Signage," *Public Services Quarterly* 10, no. 2 (April 2014): 67–95.
9. Maureen L. Mackenzie and James P. Smith, "How Does the Library Profession Grow Managers? It Doesn't—They Grow Themselves," *Advances in Librarianship* 33 (2011): 51–71.
10. Robert P. Holley, "Providing LIS Students with Management Skills," *Journal of Library Administration* 56, no. 5 (2016): 638–46.
11. Colleen S. Harris-Keith, "The Relationship between Academic Library Department Experience and Perceptions of Leadership Skill Development Relevant to Academic Library Directorship," *Journal of Academic Librarianship* 41, no. 3 (May 2015): 246–63.
12. American Library Association, *Standards for Proficiencies for Instruction Librarians and Coordinators: A Practical Guide* (2008).
13. David Shumaker, "Who Let the Librarians Out?," *Reference and User Services Quarterly* 48, no. 3 (Spring 2009): 239–42.

14. Brian Brim and Jim Asplund, "Driving Engagement by Focusing on Strengths," accessed November 18, 2016, www.gallup.com/businessjournal/124214/Driving-Engagement-Focusing-Strengths.aspx.

15. Sean Cordes and Brian Clark, "Business Process Management and the 'New' Library Instruction Navigating Technology and Collaboration," College and Research Libraries News 70, no. 5 (2009): 272–75.

16. Sara Ahmed, *On Being Included: Racism and Diversity in Institutional Life* (Durham: Duke University Press, 2012).

17. Fariborz Damanpour, Kathryn A. Szabat, and William M. Evan, "The Relationship between Types of Innovation and Organizational Performance," *Journal of Management Studies* 26, no. 6 (November 1989): 587–601.

FURTHER READINGS

Ahmed, Sara. *On Being Included: Racism and Diversity in Institutional Life.* Durham: Duke University Press, 2012.

American Library Association. *Standards for Proficiencies for Instruction Librarians and Coordinators: A Practical Guide.* 2008.

Brim, Brian, and Jim Asplund. "Driving Engagement by Focusing on Strengths." Accessed November 18, 2016. www.gallup.com/businessjournal/124214/Driving-Engagement-Focusing-Strengths.aspx.

Cordes, Sean, and Brian Clark. "Business Process Management and the 'New' Library Instruction Navigating Technology and Collaboration." *College and Research Libraries News* 70, no. 5 (2009): 272–75.

Damanpour, Fariborz, Kathryn A. Szabat, and William M. Evan. "The Relationship between Types of Innovation and Organizational Performance." *Journal of Management Studies* 26, no. 6 (November 1989): 587–601.

Harris-Keith, Colleen S. "The Relationship between Academic Library Department Experience and Perceptions of Leadership Skill Development Relevant to Academic Library Directorship." *Journal of Academic Librarianship* 41, no. 3 (May 2015): 246–63.

Hess, Amanda Nichols. "Scheduling Research Consultations with YouCanBook.Me." *College and Research Libraries News* 75, no. 9 (October 2014): 510–13.

Holley, Robert P. "Providing LIS Students with Management Skills." *Journal of Library Administration* 56, no. 5 (2016): 638–46.

Hurley, Christine A. "Fixed vs. Flexible Scheduling in School Library Media Centers: A Continuing Debate." *Library Media Connection* 23, no. 3 (2004) 36–41.

Lackie, Robert J., and Edward M. Corrado. "The Multi-purpose Library Computer Lab: Tips and Techniques for Successful Operation and Management." *College and Undergraduate Libraries* 8, no. 2 (2001): 27–51.

Mackenzie, Maureen L., and James P. Smith. "How Does the Library Profession Grow Managers? It Doesn't—They Grow Themselves." *Advances in Librarianship* 33 (2011): 51–71.

McGregor, Joy. "Flexible Scheduling: Implementing an Innovation." *School Library Media Research* 9 (2006).

Polger, Mark Aaron, and Amy F. Stempler. "Out with the Old, in with the New: Best Practices for Replacing Library Signage." *Public Services Quarterly* 10, no. 2 (April 2014): 67–95.

Shumaker, David. "Who Let the Librarians Out?" *Reference and User Services Quarterly* 48, no. 3 (Spring 2009): 239–42.

Staley, Laura A. "Using Survey Sites for Information Literacy Scheduling and Teaching." *College and Undergraduate Libraries* 14, no. 3 (2007): 103–6.

Stelk, Roger, and Suping Lu. "Eight Days a Week: The Art of Reference Desk Scheduling." *Reference Librarian* no. 59 (October 1997): 37.

Woodard, Beth S., and Lisa Janicke Hinchliffe. "Technology and Innovation in Library Instruction Management." *Journal of Library Administration* 36, no. 1/2 (2002): 39–55.

Communications

Introduction

Few jokes grow as old to a librarian as the one that starts, "Oh, you're a librarian? Guess you're going to shush me!" Although serious inroads have been made into the profession in terms of ensuring that old stereotypes and tropes have begun to fade (in part due to the work of librarians like Nicole Pagowsky of Librarian Wardrobe and Erin Downey Howerton and Bobbi Newman of This is What a Librarian Looks Like) or at least be replaced with more accurate ones, there is still some truth to the fact that people who go into librarianship tend to be more reserved and introverted.[1] As part of the information literacy trade, instruction coordinators come into contact with large portions of the university and act as the ambassadors of their programs on many fronts. This level of interaction involves multiple forms of communication, and public services and instruction tend to draw librarians who are slightly more extroverted than others. No matter where an instruction coordinator may fall between introversion or extroversion, this chapter provides standardized formats and methods of contact and communication with the specific areas you will come into regular contact with. To avoid redundancy with other sections of the book, this chapter focuses on areas of communication as they arise through the work of coordination and how they can be used to differing degrees of efficacy.

A Note on Preferences

As you go about your day-to-day work as a coordinator, you will develop your own personal style for communicating with various groups. You may already be aware of these preferences. Some people hate to use the phone, and others refuse to commit anything to writing, preferring to do everything face-to-face. While there is no one universal "right" way to communicate, bear in mind that your preferences may not necessarily match those of the people you are trying to work with. One thing to consider is that using multiple forms of communication can help alleviate accessibility issues or make it easier on others.[2] Some people prefer to use email because they have trouble hearing on telephones, and others prefer the phone because they may have trouble reading email on small screens or perhaps have difficulty accessing their email from off campus. Whatever the preference, likely someone prefers a different method for a reason. Try your best to accommodate those who have different preferences than you, and bear in mind that all these methods seek to teach students. As long as the end goal is making sure people get together and learn about information literacy, it should all be well.

Regardless of the style you choose, as instruction coordinator, you will have to deal with a host of different groups daily. Finding a style that makes you comfortable is one small step toward making day-to-day interactions pleasant and joyful.

Email

Like it or not, email is a huge part of your life as an instruction coordinator. Finding a way to manage it and use it effectively can help you be a better leader. We have come a long way from interdepartmental memos to the spam and clutter that finds its way into our inboxes every day. To sort through what is worthwhile and what is not is to deal with an almost Sisyphean task—so much so that the concept of Inbox Zero[3] has come along in popular culture as a method for organizing inbox clutter. The idea, brought about by Merlin Mann, is to treat the inbox as a to-do list, with action items needing quick responses as they come in and an expectation that if more information is needed, people will ask for it. Although it is an admirable method, it does not always address what librarians need from email. One librarian reports a method wherein she tries not to send email to any person in her office whom she can talk to in person. Managing email is a task that takes up a not insignificant portion of most librarians' days, so for most readers, this information should seem familiar.

Other Email Management Options

- RAFT (Refer, Act, File, or Toss)
- OHIO (Only Handle It Once)

Although some letters and memos do not merit a response or require no more than a glancing nod, for those we do need to acknowledge, a subtle countdown begins once they arrive in our inboxes. Most business communications—specifically those in which a teaching faculty member has requested an instruction session—must be replied to in a timely manner at minimum. They may not need a full response, but if you at least give some form of reply, along the lines of "Thank you for your request to have a class taught at [day/time]. I am currently looking to see how we can fulfill this request. I will be in touch shortly," this acknowledges the specific request and that there will be more to come. A request that lies in your inbox without any form of reply or acknowledgement can create ill will with the teaching faculty. If your department receives a flood of requests at certain times of the year, it could be worth looking into generative response statements. Certainly during the start of the semester, we all get busy, and teaching faculty are known to ignore our helpful guidelines about making requests before the semester starts. If we try to apply a form of equalization and making them "wait" Things can quickly become unmanageable.

Often instruction programs rely on a departmental email for all requests, and the coordinator is the one who does the majority of managing this account. If there are multiple people with access to the account, be wary of the many tiered approach to filing, deleting and response times for the emails. While in the best-case scenario everyone works in concert with requests as they come in, most frequently, the email tends to be managed in practice by one, or have emails languish in the inbox as others debate on who should respond. I recommend acting as the primary manager of this account if you should have one at your institution, and designating perhaps one person as back up in cases of need.

When thinking about instruction coordination, it can often be too simplistic to think of instruction as being only one particular type. The most common form of instruction remains the face-to-face classroom experience, but there are many variations of instruction. Some librarians go so far as to view "reference" as instruction at the point of need. When considering how to use email for library instruction, think also of distance education and embedded courses. These may require heavy email communication, particularly for those students who may not be able to easily get to the library's physical location. Often this work is nested within an institutional learning management system (LMS) such as Blackboard, Canvas, or Moodle. Each of these systems has its own specific features and problems, and because LMS can vary by institution, I will not go into the specifics of how to navigate them. A general rule of thumb is to check messages and discussion boards frequently. Knowing the course syllabus allows you to know when things must be posted on the discussion boards as well as major due dates for papers and exams so that you can prepare for when you'll likely get questions from students. Students may not immediately feel comfortable reaching out to a course librarian in the beginning of the class, so the onus will be on you to find ways to make these students feel comfortable around you, particularly because, depending on the module, some may be distance-learning students who may never meet you face-to-face. The online environment has created a situation where the rules for interaction are in some ways still in flux, and it can be fascinating and yet a very vivid work in progress for those trying to figure out the best way to take advantage of the system. In cases like these, some librarians choose to film short videos of themselves and embed them in the course. A number of free and low-cost resources are available for these videos, such as Kaltura or Panopto. Given the capabilities of many cell phones and webcams at this point, a number of librarians have chosen to upload videos using their own technology. Depending on how these photos and videos will be used and displayed, especially if these items might be digitally preserved down the road for the university, the instructor may want to check on the specifications of the files they are uploading.

Social Media

Each library embraces a different policy toward social media. In some cases, libraries have effectively leveraged their social media accounts into ways to attract new patrons and provide a new form of outreach to those who might not have been aware of programming and collections. Others have found more lackluster results and feel that because of a lack of followers, their posts go into a void, to be "liked" or seen only by the library staff, who already know about the events and collections. In rarer instances, allowing the public to provide feedback in such a relatively uncontrolled environment has created public relations disasters as libraries grapple to understand how to combat an influx of negative comments and posts. Although most of these interactions are based on patrons' negative experiences along the lines of fines for lost books or being charged twice for expensive printing jobs, these are all issues that need to be dealt with quickly when they appear on social media.

Without spending too much time on each particular social media format, think first about what will be accomplished by creating social media accounts for your instruction program. If it is hard to define why these accounts are needed, it will be hard to manage the account if only because who would want to follow it. Likewise, think if this an instruction-specific account or related to the whole library, which will promote some instruction items. One reason instruction librarians get involved with social media is to be able to reach their students better. Some embedded instruction librarians create a Facebook group that their students can join so that they can ask questions without the hassle of a more formal communication method. Similar methods involve creating a class hashtag and allowing students to post on

Twitter or Instagram to have discussions that might feel uncomfortable in class. As an instruction coordinator, before giving the go-ahead, have a process in place for approving or denying new techniques. Although it may be class specific and generated with good intentions, the actions of one librarian (even a well-meaning one) can affect an entire department.

Part of why social media has had such successful buy-in from groups around the world is that the services rarely have an upfront cost, and what can pass as a quick diversion also happens to provide outreach and marketing that can reach groups that are often the hardest to reach. However, although the service may not have an initial cost, many libraries face an unseen human cost in terms of lost labor and money spent on advertising or a subscription fee to upgrade the service. On the flip side, because it is so easy and quick to buy into, it can be incredibly hard to make it into a habit or practice that gives form to those same users who would see the postings. You might want to drive home a purpose for the postings when helping other instruction librarians think of how and what to post. A lack of purpose can make some users cautious about what they should post or why they should post at all. Working either alone or preferably with your team, think critically about what purpose social media will serve for your program. Besides simply alerting patrons about locations, closures, and so on, you might consider highlighting specific lesson plans or even incorporating student work. Many instructors assume that their students are already using these services, so they may as well bring the lesson onto the platform and have student and teacher use it together to create meaningful use of it. This is a great idea, but when doing so, again, there needs to be not just a lesson plan but a purpose. For example, think of discerning "fake news" from real news on Facebook and Twitter. Have students sort through trending articles, look at the sources for each article, and evaluate headlines and why they draw attention. When you create lessons that take advantage of the resources and highlight aspects a student may not have been exposed to yet, you add purpose while using the platforms to advance your own instruction goals. Weak use of social media relies on giving users crumbs of information that can be found in other locations and expecting them to be engaged and fascinated by these stale crumbs. To create continuous engagement, provide new information and discuss what types of lessons are going on in the library. This creates a feedback loop where those who are not actively using the library for its information literacy programs may see these postings and want to collaborate with your library on future endeavors. Yes, there is a real and understandable risk to making public the creative work of instructors who may be concerned about digital theft of their creations. There are a few ways to address these concerns. First, I would encourage usage rights to be posted with any lesson plan. This could simply mean acknowledging that the lesson is part of the Creative Commons or not posting the work of instructors who may be compiling information for their own research until after publication. There are sites like Project CORA which actively encourage instruction librarians to post creative commons lesson plans, and sharing on places like social media and the web allows you to be part of the greater conversation of instruction. Publication times with journals and books can take far longer than the usual academic semester cycle, but then, even using these platforms meaningfully to highlight lessons, there will be times when there may be a perceived lack of content. It's wise to have projects queued up and waiting in the wings to be posted after publication should you need something to post about.

Many professors as well as librarians have tried to find ways to bring social media into the classroom by creating either a class hashtag or group page that can be referred back to many times throughout the class. With due respect to these instructors seeking better ways to engage their students, this method requires buy-in into a system that students may not necessarily be using or willing to use in an academic setting, as experienced by Peter Tiernan, when a third of his students chose not to use Twitter, citing a lack of interest in the platform.[4] A pro of using social media is that it can encourage students who may feel intimidated by speaking up in class to voice opinions that might otherwise go unheard.

Although lesson plans typically do not need to be done consistently or vetted by the instruction coordinator, in the case of social media use, it can be helpful for all instructors to be on the same page to help maintain a standard. Often instruction coordinators need to speak up when they notice that a professor's assignment does not meet information literacy needs. Content professors may be eager to create a library assignment that involves using social media platforms, but sometimes these have very little practical value to the library or the students in terms of meaningfully teaching information literacy. If you notice a conversation like this is about to take place between a content professor and one of your instructors, please step in and offer some advice on how to improve the lesson or even clarify the goals of the assignment. As I have stressed throughout the book, we are not duty bound to teach the first idea that comes to a professor's mind. Rather, it should be a dialogue of figuring out the goals for each class and creating lesson plans to reflect them.

Although all lesson plans need to be updated periodically for content freshness and to ensure that the lesson still works and applies to the students who will be using it, for those who incorporate social media in particular, it is useful to refresh yourself on the platforms used within a week or so of teaching the course. Social media sites are prone to page redesigns and functionality changes that can happen overnight with little or no advance notice to the end users. Keeping this in mind is a good caveat for those who may otherwise be caught unaware as they go into a lesson plan. Having to hastily rework a lesson plan on the fly due to changed circumstances is a terrible feeling, and it will show in how the class receives the lesson.

How to Know When It's Time to Update a Lesson Plan

Age

- Establishing when the lesson was first created helps provide a guideline for decisions.
- Not all old lessons are bad, but they may have incorrect facts in them.

Format

- Depending on the resources used, screenshots may need to be updated or have broken links cleaned out or updated.

Exposure

- How many students at the university have experienced this lesson as is?

Interest

- Does the instructor still enjoy teaching the lesson? Does it involve parts without updates that may frustrate a teacher?

Relevancy

- Does the lesson still pertain to the overall learning objectives of the classes?

As with email, social media requires a quick response time. With email, most people expect that it may take longer to reply, as most people are not always at their desks and may require time and thought to reply to an in-depth request, but they do expect a response. With social media, not only is a response expected, but it is expected during a much shorter amount of time, in part because we tend to carry personal devices at all times. Tablets and cell phones can quickly send out updates and with very little thought behind them. The twenty-four-hour reply time frame is perhaps the longest possible for social media, and even that gets a little toothy. The preference is for replies to come within the hour or, barring that, within the day—usually twelve hours or so. Rightfully so, this may seem intimidating to those who have other job functions besides managing a social media account. It is not a task to be taken on lightly.[5] Look at peer institutions and see if they have stated social media policies or a social media manager who would be willing to discuss policy and technique. Instruction librarians are often the public-facing members of the library staff whom students see and react to the most. Aside from circulation and information desks, we are the faces the students will remember and associate with the idea of a library (particularly an academic one). While this may make you feel glad or nervous, remember also that social media encompasses not just what we post on our own channels but also what our students are posting about us. Posts made about us tend not to be standard quick reference questions but closer to complaints and jokes about the nature of our physical space. A quick search of what is currently being posted by students in my Twitter area reveals students talking about sleeping in the library, sneaking food in, and meeting friends. This is not unusual and does not typically warrant any interaction from the library, unless a specific policy is in place to respond and reach out to everyone mentioning the library.[6]

Many have commented on the fact that there are so many social media channels to use. Even in the time since this book was first began, trends among popular apps have come and gone, so it can feel disingenuous to write a print tome on social media. Many libraries feel as if they have to chase after trends in social media, hopping from one channel to another. Especially if one person is managing these accounts, it can feel burdensome to make sure that each channel is updated and has unique content. This can result not only in multiple accounts being made with the additional work needed for each channel but also to consciously think about the fact that many institutions have stratified and separated out their accounts by service or specialization. Often a "parent" account represents the larger institution and smaller "child" accounts, and many universities want to be aware of what accounts have been created by which departments. Check in with the marketing and communications offices to see if they have a house policy that can be applied to the library accounts.

Unless there is something truly important to get across, these accounts should not be using and publishing the same content. At this point in time, social media is not really a "new" concept to most people, and it is hard to argue that only youths are using it, so likely your library already has one or more social media accounts and a social media policy in place to enforce them. As the instruction coordinator, you need to figure out what parts of instruction need to be advertised through these mediums. For example, an instruction-based account could post profiles of the instruction librarians, reminders of classes about to be taught, photos of particularly engaging classes (think group work activities, work on whiteboards, etc.), student interviews, or highlights of particular instruction products, such as a citation manager or a highly used database tool.

Telephone

Depending on how old you are, your attitude toward the telephone may differ wildly from that of your colleagues. Of those groups that grew up with cell phones and internet versus those who learned to use them in adulthood (in order to spare feelings and wide generalization, specific generations will go unnamed), each has its own personal perceptions about the phone. As instruction coordinators learn the traits of their specific contacts, it is worth remembering that some people are deeply uncomfortable when talking on the phone, and others love it. I have met professors who refuse to be contacted by phone for various reasons—perhaps they are never in their offices or simply prefer taking the time to write out their thoughts clearly before they reply in an email.

Other issues to be considered involve cell phones. Some departments and librarians have company-provided cell phones for their work. By nature, cell phones, which have applications and a high degree of personalization and are always by our sides, allow for informality. If you have already established an informal professional tone, this might be OK, but remember that when you use a company-provided product, you are working. As the device becomes a daily part of your life, it is easy to forget that this is not something you purchased or use for your own enjoyment. This is not even in reference to major offenses, like taking private photos or sharing rude things about coworkers. Rather, the mere act of being comfortable in a position or role with those you are emailing can lead your communications to be relaxed as well. In a sense, this is good! After all, no one wants to communicate in a purely stiff and formalized manner, but an awareness of that comfort can sometimes help curb impulses. Finding your professional tone and balancing it with your true personality can sometimes be the biggest test for new instruction coordinators trying to find their footing, especially when they are still figuring out the rules in a new location.

Establishing Boundaries

One of the primary tasks of communication is to realize that in order to get a message across, a fair amount of listening from both parties is involved. Coordinators can talk up a storm and send out as many messages as they like to their particular groups, but from time to time, some groups will be unwilling to listen for whatever reason. Although some instruction coordinators have supervision over their instructors, a great deal more lack supervision over this group. And telling the difference between someone who is unwilling to listen or work and someone who has reached his or her course overload line can be difficult at times.

What brings up these problems? In some cases, they are caused by easy-to-solve issues such as a difference in communication style or scheduling. Perhaps one person only works nights and weekends and never really has the time or energy to arrive for a Monday-morning meeting. Or perhaps someone is more of a linear thinker rather than focused on abstract concepts. These communication breakdowns are some of the easier ones to solve because they ask us to step outside of our comfort zones and tackle the topic in a new way. Those based on personality differences are broader and in some ways more complicated. They are also the challenges the instruction coordinator is most likely to face. One of the best ways to figure out where people are concerning their ideas on information literacy and the world in general can be to sit down with them face-to-face and get a better impression of what they want. Finding a way to grab content professors' time and attention can be tricky, but even something as simple as inviting them out for a cup of coffee or tea can help give a lighter sense of structure to awkward conversations, such as when they have lessons or assignments prepared that do not help their students or need to be tweaked in other ways. Sometimes even the act of being on neutral ground can have an unconscious calming effect on both parties.

Perhaps one of the more frequent problems that can arise is when library instruction does not go as planned and you receive negative feedback from a content professor about an instructor's lesson. Dealing with negative feedback is just plain hard for all parties. You have students who may not have gotten the right information they needed to perform their research. Then the content professor may feel that valuable class time was wasted by poor instruction that did not meet their goals for the class. Librarian instructors can feel as though they are being personally attacked due to factors that may be out of their control, so it's important for the instruction coordinator to find a way to minimize damage. The longer you wait to reach out to all involved parties, the more likely the situation will not be repaired as you would prefer. Yes, there are absolutely times when all parties need a cooling-off period, but usually this should be limited to a twenty-four-hour time span at most. To wait any longer is to make the content professor or instruction librarian feel as though their concerns are not valid or appreciated. With most issues, it is critical to get each party's perspectives. In the best-case scenario, these situations arise from a simple breakdown in communication, where each party came into the class expecting a different type of lesson or research. If your library is already using a system of observation, using the same post observation self-reflection techniques can help you analyze what went wrong and how it could be corrected in future classes.

Students are not frequently the users who will complain to the library about poor instruction, even though they are the ones who are most acutely affected. In some cases, particularly in smaller classes, it may be worth reaching out to the students to offer one-on-one instruction or even figure out if they can be helped. Student evaluations of the class are the most common way an instruction coordinator will find out feedback from a student, and many times these evaluation forms do not have a way for instructors to follow up. The inability to make amends can be deeply frustrating. Instructors can remedy the situation by advertising that they are willing to meet after class, but some professors may naturally be suspicious of librarians essentially warning the class that the experience might not go well. Instead, instructors might make a blanket offering for students to come greet them after class and discuss whatever is on their minds. Other libraries have locked comment boxes outside their instruction spaces with options for people to submit advice with their names attached if they so choose. The use of this appears to be mixed at best, though. Overall, our feedback on our instruction is extremely limited across most institutions, and only the most egregious cases rise to the top. We can use the ways mentioned to improve ourselves in thoughtful and reflective ways.

Communication in Practice

It takes an incredible amount of time and reflection to communicate with the students, plan and edit lessons, assess performance, grade, etc. —Chelsea Stripling

In my experience, a huge part of this job is diplomacy and learning how to communicate differently with different kinds of people—administrators, students, librarians, faculty, etc. So much of this job is persuading—whether asking people to work with you, adopt certain practices, or teach classes they may not want to teach. —Elizabeth Galoozis

Gender

The ways in which we talk to one another can be as varied as the stars, but one issue to be aware of as we speak to our colleagues is that sometimes our messages can be amplified or diluted by the very aspect of gender. Consider that communication can be affected by many aspects, including how we portray and receive information. Some librarians noted that they felt as though content professors did not listen to them as fully or responded to them with respect depending on the combined factors of age and gender. Although we can rarely change the perceptions of others through overt and direct actions, there are other ways to make an impression and reframe our perspectives. Sweetman focuses on reframing our perspectives and looking at linguistic differences, such as overuse of "I'm sorry" by women, verbal uptick, or fry.[7] Another concept that comes up frequently is that of "mansplaining," wherein a man often condescendingly explains to a woman a topic she is already well-versed in. Being aware of these different types of communication can help us, if not fix the problem, then at least be aware of what is happening and create our own defenses or solutions.

The Twitter hashtag #libleadgender documents the experiences of those who have felt the influence of their gender as they have performed their roles. With a variety of voices adding to the weekly conversation, the hashtag—created and led by Jessica Olin and Michelle Millet after their original article dealing with gender and leadership in libraries[8]—centers on a theme and set of questions (moderated by a volunteer) that have been chosen ahead of time to let users discuss their experiences and thoughts on the topic. In particular, for instruction coordinators who may feel that they lack supervisory experience or lack peers to speak to about their problems, this can be a great forum for those looking for feedback and help in the area. Sometimes participating in the conversation can be intimidating, especially for those who may not be used to the rhythm or the best platform to view a hashtag conversation, but even the act of listening in on the conversation can illuminate issues.

Conclusion

There are many methods of communication, and instruction coordinators will likely need to employ all of them at some point, but rather than getting hung up on the newest and greatest or perfecting the art of using them well, focus instead on making sure that there are no loose strings and that all communication effectively closes the loop. People who are valued as good communicators are not necessarily the best orators, but they do excel at knowing who to tell what information to and when. There can be power in a curated reveal. Even focusing on what others are saying can speak volumes about you as a communicator, because with luck, you will perceive needs and find ways to meet them. It is an art that takes time and practice, but it is worth it in the long haul.

Academic Season Communications

Fall Semester

The "official" start of the academic year, fall semester tends to be the busiest for instruction across most institutions, as a majority of introductory-level freshman classes are taught during this time and a new year brings increased motivation to schedule instruction.

AUGUST

- Generate information packets for new faculty.
- Encourage faculty to book instruction early.

SEPTEMBER

- Perform pre- and postinstruction follow-up with instructors.
- Create handouts.

OCTOBER

- Midterms

NOVEMBER

- Begin writing letters of recommendation or make professional resume and CV touchups for end-of-year job performance evaluations for both yourself and your instructors.

DECEMBER

- Finals
  - Although little instruction takes place during this time, consider offering students an instruction lab as a study area or sending a newsletter or a word of thanks to all teaching faculty your department worked with during the semester.

Winter Break / Intersession

Typically, winter break is a slow time during the academic season when little gets accomplished. Due to an above-average amount of vacations and holidays, this may not be the best time to start major projects involving multiple partners. However, it can be an excellent time to do soft rollouts and test practices that may not always have the best reactions from students. Looking to try a new intercom or bullhorn? Go for it!

During winter intersession, usually a small amount of abbreviated classes are being taught online and in person. Depending on your instruction goals, it may be important for you to reach out to online classes. Typically, this is done through embedding and email and chat reference contact. If this is something that will be done with instruction during the winter, make sure that a librarian dedicated to that class is available. If that person is planning vacations or breaks that would take away from class time, reflect on how to teach in a timely manner. You could include several premade assignments and prompts that could be graded later.

Spring Semester

Instruction happens in spring semester, but you may find that the pace and type of class that comes into the library vary from the classes you see in fall semester. In part, this is due to a smaller amount of beginning-level classes being taught as well as a mistaken belief by some professors that by that point, students will have already been to the library and know it all.

JANUARY

- Weather can effect class participation, and depending on the location of your institution, be prepared for classes that arrive late or have difficulty making it to the library. This is a season where I encourage instructors to wait or give wiggle time before launching into instruction.
- At the beginning of the spring semester, look for transfer students and spring starters. These students likely missed freshman orientation at your institution and may need a refresher for the specifics.

FEBRUARY

- February and March classes are similar to those taught in September and October of the previous year, but this is also a time when follow-up classes are rampant, and you may get requests to repeat past lesson plans or build on prior sessions.

MARCH

- This is a transitional time of the year for most locales, and certainly it's a time to focus on midterms and how the library can benefit teachers and students who may need extra time or training. Sometimes it may be worth approaching a professor at the beginning of the semester to ask if he or she would like to create a directed study prep session with the library.

APRIL

- After spring break, you should see a reduction in one-shot instruction but a rise in student body numbers in the building.

MAY

- At the close of the semester, you should not experience a high volume of instruction. However, May is the start of a heavy conference time. Expect that many people will be out of the office at national conferences and events. If you have a small pool of instructors, you might need to choose who to keep back during what times of year. For a list of potential conferences, see chapter 3.

Summer Break / Intersession

Unlike winter break, when there are either no classes or highly abbreviated classes, summer often has a few routine classes on the roster. Universities and colleges often have visiting students from high schools or other universities as part of camps or local conferences. This time can be used for a small amount of one-shots.

JUNE

- This month continues conference season, and while conferences can happen at any time of the year, there is a high concentration during the summer months.
- Summer classes have a shorter timeline, so replies to requests for instruction need to be especially quick. If response is delayed because of a holiday or personal vacation, we can risk not having a chance to reschedule at a future date.

JULY

- This is understandably a slow month for instruction. The types of instruction that take place in July tend to be orientations for incoming groups of students, ranging from student athletes who have arrived early for training to those in specialized and intensive training programs where study can be rigorous. Aside from orientations, this is a great month for training with instruction librarians and reviewing lesson plans.

Rinse and repeat!

NOTES

1. J. A. Bartlett, "New and Noteworthy: Coming to Terms with Librarian Stereotypes and Self-Image," *Library Leadership and Management* (Online) 29 (2014): 1–5.
2. Shupei Yuan, Syed A. Hussain, Kayla D. Hales, and Shelia R. Cotten, "What Do They Like? Communication Preferences and Patterns of Older Adults in the United States: The Role of Technology," *Educational Gerontology* 42, no. 3 (2016): 163–74.
3. M. Mann, "How Can I Tame My Overflowing Inbox?," *Popular Science* 269 (December 2006): 127.
4. P. Tiernan, "A Study of the Use of Twitter by Students for Lecture Engagement and Discussion," *Education and Information Technologies* 19, no. 4 (2014): 673–90. http://dx.doi.org/10.1007/s10639-012-9246-4.
5. I. Xie and J. Stevenson, "Social Media Application in Digital Libraries," *Online Information Review* 38, no. 4 (2014): 502.
6. Lynette Schimpf, "Creating a Social Media Strategy at Your Library," *Florida Libraries* 57, no. 1 (Spring 2014): 13–16.
7. K. Sweetman, "Workplace Expectations for Today's Library," Young Adult Library Services 14, no. 4 (2016): 40–43.
8. Jessica Olin and Michelle Millet, "Gendered Expectations for Leadership in Libraries," *In the Library with the Lead Pipe* (blog), accessed July 14, 2017, www.inthelibrarywiththeleadpipe.org/2015/libleadgender/.

FURTHER READINGS

Bartlett, J. A. "New and Noteworthy: Coming to Terms with Librarian Stereotypes and Self-Image." *Library Leadership and Management* (Online) 29 (2014): 1–5.

Olin, Jessica, and Michelle Millet. "Gendered Expectations for Leadership in Libraries." *In the Library with the Lead Pipe* (blog). Accessed July 14, 2017. www.inthelibrarywiththeleadpipe.org/2015/libleadgender/.

Mann, M. "How Can I Tame My Overflowing Inbox?" *Popular Science* 269 (December 2006): 127.

Schimpf, Lynette. "Creating a Social Media Strategy at Your Library." *Florida Libraries* 57, no. 1 (Spring 2014): 13–16.

Sweetman, K. "Workplace Expectations for Today's Library." *Young Adult Library Services* 14, no. 4 (2016): 40–43.

Tiernan, P. "A Study of the Use of Twitter by Students for Lecture Engagement and Discussion." *Education and Information Technologies* 19, no. 4 (2014): 673–90. http://dx.doi.org/10.1007/s10639-012-9246-4.

Xie, I., and J. Stevenson. "Social Media Application in Digital Libraries." *Online Information Review* 38, no. 4 (2014): 502.

Yuan, Shupei, Syed A. Hussain, Kayla D. Hales, and Shelia R. Cotten. "What Do They Like? Communication Preferences and Patterns of Older Adults in the United States: The Role of Technology." *Educational Gerontology* 42, no. 3 (2016): 163–74.

6

Assessment

Introduction

The assessment of library instruction is a tricky topic, not one that people readily jump into. The language of assessment can be confusing, and it can reveal things we do not necessarily want to see. Even to mention what is frequently referred to by some academics as "the A word" is to make people upset. This is not to say that assessment is inherently bad. It is rather to reflect on the fact that when assessment is good, it is very good, and when it is bad, it can be very ugly. As accreditation has become more prominent within academia, assessment has gained importance. Accreditation has been around for decades, as has assessment. Learning to meet the needs of an accrediting body, an institutional administration, and perhaps even your library association can be a delicate balancing act, but it is doable. As I interviewed instruction coordinators for this book, one of the most common complaints and frustrations stemmed from a need for assessment. Many said they had been unaware of how much assessment would be required for this position, and they had a real desire to learn better skills related to instructional design and assessment. In some cases, coordinators felt that assessment took up major amounts of their time, taking them away from the parts of the job that they actually enjoyed. Others felt pushed toward performing assessment but lacked an understanding of how the information could be gathered or applied. For those who enjoy assessment, it can be unsettling to hear these frequent complaints about it. There is no doubt that frustrations can come along with assessment, but at the core of assessment is valuable research that can help you be a better librarian and serve your students better. Using this information allows you to influence yourself and others going forward to bring a form of assessment into the classroom that ultimately will help coordinators meet goals and provide constructive feedback.

Gathering Information

Create an Assessment Plan

Serious assessment that provides values and information that you can use well into the future takes careful preparation and thought.[1] The following are several schools of thought on how to map out your assessment plan; many follow a similar pattern:

- use state expected outcomes/expectations
- identify areas where outcomes are addressed
- use methodology/determine how to assess
- collect baseline information
- interpret

Each of these steps involves a deliberate thought process that identifies what areas most need assessment and also helps inform the next steps of the process. Incorporated into this process is also a realistic estimate of how much time and energy will be needed to accomplish each task. This is not to imply that all assessment projects will take months or years but rather to forewarn those who think assessment can be done at the spur of the moment; in practice, assessment takes time and application. Each step relies on generalized knowledge of what can be gathered from the measurement tool. In particular, analyzing the baseline information available to you before you begin a project can help you compare and figure out growth and measurement methods later in the project. Gathering data for assessment is great and, in many ways, one of the more fun aspects of the procedure, but without the information that gives meaning to it, assessment can leave the instruction coordinator with raw data that are open to conjecture but contain no inherent meaning.

> Instruction is not quantifiable in the same way as other departments. Compared to collections or ILL [interlibrary loan] or e-resources or circulation or any other department that is constantly churning out statistical analyses, from the outside instruction is opaque. How do you quantify the six hours you consulted with a faculty member on an assignment, the four hours you spent preparing for a course, or the two hours you spent helping a student learn EndNote? —Lane Wilkinson, University of Tennessee, Knoxville

Self-assessment and assessment of where your information literacy program rests within the university curriculum can help guide the way you develop future assessments. The Association of College and Research Libraries (ACRL) Instruction Sessions workbook Analyzing Your Instruction Environment[2] is one incredibly useful guided method for instruction coordinators who have not yet had the experience of assessing an instruction program (or those who have not performed assessment in a while). Primarily consisting of checklists and questions, you can use it as a framework to help you see the state of your program. As you go through the lists, areas and items of note should make themselves clear to you either because there is no answer for them or because there is a perceived lack of need for them. This is not an activity you can do quickly or at the spur of the moment; rather, it must be done thoughtfully over the course of a semester or your own specific time frame. The effort will reward you with a great perspective of where to take the instruction program in the future. Many times, the work of assessment will seem recursive, and it will feel as if you are treading similar waters, but part of what makes assessment useful is that it allows us new insights into the road ahead. As Lane Wilkinson mentioned, it can initially seem as though not much data can be gathered from instruction, but the beauty of designing your own assessment measures is that the methods you choose will make clear the details that you may have always sensed about your instruction yet have been unable to show to others.

Some believe that pretesting is vital to a properly run assessment. For example, if you are using a new instrument, it is wise to run sample data before the first real run so that you can get a sense of how the process works. Even though it may be just a test, thinking of the information received as real allows you to see any potential flaws in the results you gather, such as whether the results are what the test was designed to gather or whether this information actually informs you of new information. One of the biggest frustrations is to sift through assessment results and realize that the information you are looking for is not there because the measurements did not ask for or search for that information. Trial runs can prevent these frustrations.

Scenario: Assessment in Action

In a small library instruction team, two instructors want to find out how the English 201 students did on their papers after instruction. With the help of two content professors in the English department, the librarians ask to see the final papers for the students in each class. In the control class, no library instruction was given, and in the other class, library instruction was given to the students. The final papers are compared to see the differences in bibliographies or other specific markers, like specific resources cited.

Many variations and modifications can be made to this assessment, including options where a content professor may be teaching more than one section of the same course. This allows a better sense of control. After the assessment has concluded, feel free to send an executive summary to the content professor so that he or she can see the value of the library instruction as well.

Part of the appeal of a well-done assessment is that the lesson can be repeated and improved upon over time. Providing feedback to the content professor allows for a closed loop that can then be improved upon with context.

Before you even begin to gather information, the first question you must ask yourself is, What purpose will this information serve? Knowing why you need the data and what you plan to do with it will help inform both what kind of data you collect and how you do so. Sometimes the information need will be determined by a project or by institutional goals, but try to inform this with the learning outcomes the instruction team has chosen. This not only prepares you for the information you will receive during the real assessment; it also gives you time to correct any areas where the information received does not measure up or the instrument fails to perform in the anticipated way. Other than understanding the purpose of the data, also think about what you will do with your findings. Assessment for assessment's sake is what builds frustration among faculty.

How can you start assessing?

Do . . .

- keep all your data in one spot.
- talk to your IRB department.
- have clear checkpoints built in.

Don't . . .

- be too scared to start.
- assess multiple types of classes at once.
- compare yourself to others.
- try to reinvent the wheel (there are plenty of examples to draw from).

There are many valuable ways to write learning outcomes; however, when gathering data based on these learning outcomes, it is helpful to have clearly written, measurable, and definable outcomes. Much information can be pulled from instruction, but if it does not correlate with the outcome you are trying to research, what purpose did either the gathered data or the outcome serve? Good outcomes can inform how we teach and give us thoughtful perspectives on the purposes of our actions within and outside of the classroom. One way to provide meaning and definition to learning outcomes is to focus on Bloom's taxonomy.[3] This theoretical model, which has gone through several iterations, gives structure to language in three separate domains. Looking through the list, you may be able to substitute language in your former learning outcomes with something more useful. A great deal of assessment and learning outcomes rests on simply finding a way to measure and document learning by multiple means.[4] In 2013, Melissa Becher went about trying to find out just how aware instruction coordinators were of **accreditation** standards regarding information literacy for their particular institutions.[5] The results of her research showed both the strengths and the weaknesses of relying on instruction coordinators to be aware of this documentation. If you are leading an instruction program, you will want to be able to look to what your institution needs from you and your team in order to successfully help them meet their goals. Both library administration and university administration are going to be looking to you to help them meet the goals of accreditation. Knowing this, it is important to not only know your accrediting body but look through any regulations that specifically mention information literacy and see how and where information literacy will need to be addressed to the student body.

Accreditation: A process or system of providing credentials and competency to an institution by means of recognition and recommendation. Usually, this process is done by an external regulating body through a review of standards.

Often the language is written to accommodate current practices, but if you see that perhaps engineering or mathematics need to be information literate as one of their core competencies, discuss with the chairs of these departments how you can help them meet that goal. Perhaps starting in the classroom may be difficult, but if the instruction program has an online presence or course, it may be easier to gain buy-in by offering online videos or quick quizzes directed at the key subject areas that the library and the chairs have decided to focus on. These areas can even be mediated by a subject liaison with in-depth experience with the department who may know the best way to approach the department.

A number of sources and locations offer large data sets, including ones on information literacy. While these are not relative to your specific institution and needs, it can be worth monitoring their processes and examining what information they decided to collect in order to figure out how and to what scale your institution should approach collecting information for assessment. Of particular interest to the instruction coordinator is the work done by Project Information Literacy (PIL), a research organization based entirely on understanding how college-age students use information literacy skills. The reports and work from this group can help instruction coordinators shape their own assessment measures as well as better understand how students may be receiving information from the library. Where others have looked at mixed methods, such as opinion surveys, skills testing, and observed behavior and tried to find ways to merge these with known university data from departments such the Office of Institutional Research.[6] Indeed, many suggest that no one method is perfect, and in order to have good assessments, you must rely on mixed methods.[7] Consistency with data will help make the information you gather valid and vital. When you have to repeat the process, consider changing methods, but within the context of one research cycle; be consistent. When figuring out how to conduct research and assessment, part of what you are trying to establish is the length of your study. Consistency can mean different things to different people, but for the instruction coordinator, consistency at minimum requires keeping the same information for a set period of time. Over the years of your span as coordinator, the reports you turn in each year will need to have some form of consistency in terms of what information is presented and how it is presented, or else when reviewing information, it will be hard to measure progress and performance over time.

Choosing what to focus on can reflect what others are doing, and you can focus on some common themes, such as student learning outcomes, student engagement, and faculty performance. An unlimited number of areas can be studied, but focus on what you want from the assessment, and with that goal in mind, building your methods will become far easier. In some ways, once you have chosen a theme, the methods will begin to build themselves because the ways of measuring will necessarily follow what you are trying to find. Good structure builds the assessment for you, whereas those assessments that lack a strong foundation will face issues from the start.

Observation

When looking for information to gather and assess, one of the important things to consider is observational data from within the classroom. As instructors, we can assess based on our self-knowledge of how we feel a class may have gone, but getting an outsider's perspective can help us see what we might not have been as aware of. In earlier chapters, I discussed observation as a method for training new librarians so that they might be more aware of how to teach, but observation can also be used as a tool to see how students are reacting to and learning from the instructor. There are several ways to go about observing a lesson beyond simply having another person in the room watching. Since many times the professor of the class is in the room with their students, it might seem logical to ask this person to help observe your class, but resist this temptation. This person is often not skilled in the types of observation a library will need or will be busy moderating the students, so he or she will not have time to carefully observe in the way you will need. Bring in another librarian (instruction coordinators are perfect for this role if they have the time) who knows the specific goals of observation. An important issue for observers is protecting against getting drawn into the specifics of the lesson or socializing too much with the class or the course professor. Observers are not there to socialize or assist the instructor. They are merely there to watch and notate what they see. Socialization can include talking quietly with the class professor or even playing on a cell phone. In such a role, their presence needs to be almost immediately forgotten by the rest of the class.

When observers are in the classroom to analyze teaching strengths, they are watching for items such as how librarians present themselves, their speaking style, and the content they discuss and how they present it. However, in assessment-focused observation, observers might be looking at completely different categories of information. Indeed, they may be reflecting not on what the instruction librarians themselves are doing in the classroom but instead on what the students are doing with the lesson being presented to them. This focus allows assessment of factors not always caught by exams and papers. Some students are extremely good at parroting back what they hear, but direct observation reveals whether our students are attentive to specific parts of the lecture or if they have extended difficulty with a particular practice example. Do they need to pair up to figure out an assignment? Are they checking their phones or email? At what part of the lesson did the problem occur? All this information can not only help us assess our own instruction but inform the effectiveness of our strategies.

Observation takes place during the actual instruction and allows the observer to watch and describe what is happening during instruction, but it is just as important to meet up with the observer at a later time to process what he or she saw. In this way, it can take place over a long time. Ideally, this is done in a nonjudgmental fashion such that it is merely a report of what was observed not what could have been done better or differently. An instructor may certainly ask for advice or ways to improve, but that does not need to be the primary focus of the observation. As instruction coordinator, you may have to do a number of these observations due to staffing and your own expertise. The coordinator's role is to make sure that all instructors are teaching the same general themes of the preset learning outcomes for the semester or academic year. Observation can help you correct mistakes as you see them or even point out differences between the stated learning outcomes and how the class actually went. If a discrepancy should arise, be aware that this could be due to many different reasons, perhaps even the class being more capable and ready to move onto a higher concept than the instructor prepared for. A great deal of instruction is reactive to the academic skills students present in the classroom. Many times the content professors can prep us for that in advance, but sometimes we walk into these situations blind or realizing that perhaps the content professors did not have a full grasp of their students' skills. This works in both directions, of course.

New Media

Information literacy takes on different forms and wears many hats. When we think of assessment, there are the typical frameworks of who and what was being taught, but as our strategies for teaching slowly shift, we may find we need to assess other areas of instruction. For example, some have made interesting forays into learning how to assess students' use of social media channels and interpreting the information therein for content and authority.[8] Embedded librarians can look for ways to connect with students through their social media use and analyze which items from social media are worth assessing. Is it counting the number of likes, checking the quality of links posted, or even looking deeper at connections to other users and the spread of information? Determining what assessment methods and items can be taken from social media involves both understanding what will be useful for administrators and predicting what information will be around and useful years from now.

Reports

Periodically, administration will ask for reports from instruction coordinators about varied topics related to who is receiving instruction and the details therein. Before these requests come in, start by keeping good records. For every class taught by a librarian, the following information should be managed in some format by the instruction coordinator: course number, professor, location, who taught it, the number of students, the level, and any handouts or assignments that may be particularly relevant or attached to a course. Using this information, a great deal of data can be extrapolated about our teaching methods, our reach within the university, and other broader concepts we may be unaware of. Creating reports for administration also has the added benefit of making clear what the area needs and will need in the future. In particular, this is helpful for hiring and funding decisions. When your department is overwhelmed with instruction requests and librarians are finding themselves running across the university every which way trying to accommodate these requests, it is nice to have records and reports to back up your claims of needing a new hire to help. Administrators like to have information available to make informed decisions. Likewise, if you are consistently failing to get a grasp on a specific department or type of class, reports can help you figure out why. Sometimes leaders cannot fully articulate why or how certain areas need improvement, and looking at assessment reports can illuminate patterns that may not have been clear beforehand.

Assessment in the Real World

Kari Weaver is a library instruction coordinator at the University of South Carolina Aiken. She spoke about finding time for practicing assessment and gave advice on how to manage the role of coordinator along with all the other parts of the job:

> I would also strongly advise those who are required to do other duties such as reference to have a maximum amount of time spent on other such tasks spelled out in writing. There should be dedicated time included in your workflow for the administrative and creative tasks required for coordinators (i.e., scheduling, classroom maintenance, assessment design). This needs to be recognized as a core of your job responsibilities, not stuff you fit in around teaching and reference time.

In real life, assessment can get in the way of your day-to-day duties, but when your days are structured around how much time can be devoted to one area, you can find ways to not overdo any one area.

Assessment rests largely on the shoulders of statistics, and it is important to clarify what statistics are. This may seem redundant, but being clear on the fundamentals saves time in the long run. They can falsely be seen as a group of numbers or figures, but crucially, we are applying the work of the field of statistics, which deals with the presentation and interpretation of data. Therefore, when we generate our reports, we need to focus on maintaining statistical validity.[9] This is tricky if it is not a part of your day-to-day experience. Consider bringing in a pair of outside eyes or refreshing your memory by auditing a statistics course or consulting with a professor at your institution. The form of your report will generally follow the methods used for assessment, and the report can often write itself in that the values of your assessment will tell the story.

Evaluations

Class Evaluations

Frequently, a large portion of instruction assessment will involve class evaluations. Class evaluations can be helpful tools for understanding what happens in the classroom, but they can also be incredibly meaningless depending on how they are presented and structured. Class evaluations and instructor evaluations often get lumped together as a survey either handed out or presented as a link for students to fill out at the tail end of class or, with high hopes, after they have left the class. One of the major problems with this method is that class evaluations and instructor evaluations look at very different things. When they are intermixed, you lose the potential to understand more about the specifics of either, and often the evaluations become pro forma with little information that can be used for meaningful reflection and improvement.[10] An easy method to use is the pre- and posttest, which first tests what a student knows about the library or a specific resource prior to instruction and then tests them at the end of instruction on the same material to see whether there has been marked improvement. This is a summative measure of evaluation. Measurable improvement on the test is supposed to prove that the instruction worked, but as many critics of the method have argued, this often only tests quick recall and short-term memory. The tests are unable to show us how the students performed after they left the classroom and had to use the information in a real-world setting. It hardly needs to be said, but the purpose of information literacy is to create lifetime learners. These assessments help us see whether we are meeting our goals. Groups like Project Information Literacy are trying to find ways to measure information literacy success far into the future, even ten years after a student may have had library instruction. This scale of time can seem daunting, but it is possible.

Many assessment methods may seem hard or overwhelming, not because they are bad or poorly designed, but because of the limited amount of time we have with our students. In most institutions, the majority of classes taught remain one-shot classes, and while individually we can work on ways to change that, we should also look for ways to get informative data out of classes we may never get to see again.

One option is to look at their papers. We know that students usually write papers after they meet with us, so why not see the quality of their research directly reflected in the product? One-minute papers that give students the ability to provide reflective feedback on one or two directed questions can give a sense of what students perceived and wanted out of their experience.[11] Sometimes these things can vary drastically. Critics of this type of assignment say this creates needless busywork for students, but when done properly, the assignment can provide the librarian with a tremendous amount of feedback. Before you schedule classes with subject professors, ask them if they will allow you to look at the papers their students wrote after their instruction with you. Most are willing to accommodate this request. Figuring out what to do with this information after the fact is another thing. Student papers can vary drastically within specific classes based on many factors beyond simple education. To account for these differences, you need to find a way to norm the results. As instruction coordinator, be on the lookout for librarians who have a natural ability or inclination for assessment, as they will be extremely helpful as you begin a norming project. Some librarians will have never participated in a norming project before, and as coordinator, you can guide them through the process so that in the future, they can carry it out without as much hands-on direction. A rubric may have already been created, and certainly the former instruction coordinator needed to either approve or consult on its creation before it was implemented.[12] When should you create the rubric? In one sense, creating it right before you look at the papers allows the freedom to look for precisely what you want. Such desires can be limiting, though. When the rubric has been created prior to instruction, this can inform how librarians teach so that they know what they will be looking for in the papers and specifically teach toward the rubric. Rubrics created postinstruction can work, but they may not be as informative, if only because the librarians creating the rubric will need to think back on what they taught, and if they are looking at multiple classes taught by more than one librarian, they will have to hope that they all taught from roughly the same lesson plan. When the same scenario is enacted without a rubric created prior to the lesson, classes can vary wildly, with each librarian instructor believing that he or she met the criteria of the class.

Rubrics can vary greatly in what they assess and how they do so, but it is generally agreed that there are two major types of rubrics: holistic and analytic.[13] **Holistic** rubrics look at the project in its entirety, without looking at separate components, whereas **analytic** rubrics look at the individual parts of the project and sum them to obtain a total score. It is important to differentiate between rubrics and checklists as well. Often they are seen as somewhat similar, but they function differently.

Each type of rubric can provide different feedback to those using it. It is not unusual for a holistic rubric to be returned to students so that they can see what they need to work on and in some cases how to improve. Often in library instruction, we do not have the opportunity to return feedback to our students, or if we do, it is only through the class professor. So when using rubrics from the perspective of the library instruction world, we are often the students learning from our own work to see how we can improve.

Instructor Evaluations

There are a couple of ways to go about instructor evaluations. You can view them as a personal measurement tool to help instructors improve their own skills, or they can be viewed as an assessment tool to be used for furthering instructors' vitae and tenure packages. Instructor evaluations are not universally performed, and some feel that the pros do not outweigh the cons, because the results can be confusing to teaching faculty. Whatever line your library comes down on in regard to instructor evaluations, be sure to be consistent in the approach and methodical. Look to all the places an instructor is assessed, both internally from their supervisor and perhaps reappointment and tenure committee, and make sure that you are not muddying the waters with more evaluations.

Finding Good Evaluations

The following is a list of LibGuides that show an excellent use of teacher evaluations:
- Northwestern Library Instructors' Toolkit: http://libguides.northwestern
  .edu/instructiontoolkit/home/
- Bowling Green State University Librarian Toolkit for Instruction Teams:
  http://libguides.bgsu.edu/librariantoolkit/
- Claremont Colleges Library Information Literacy Habits of Mind Toolkit:
  http://libguides.libraries.claremont.edu/iltoolkit/
- Emory Libraries First-Year Composition Instructor Toolkit: http://guides
  .main.library.emory.edu/FYCToolkit/
- California State University, Fullerton: http://lib-learning.fullterton.edu
- University of Texas Libraries Information Literacy Toolkit: https://guides
  .lib.utexas.edu/toolkit

Class evaluations have the benefit of looking at what happened during a specific time period and seeing if methods could be improved. Instructor evaluations walk on a fine line between looking at a specific instructor's actions and looking for ways to improve upon them. Many classroom observation forms can also be applied to one-shots, but professors who have taught semester-long classes will have the best evaluations to work with because the university or college will already have a standardized evaluation form used by every course regardless of content. The trick when creating instructor evaluations is to create a standardized form that will accompany every instructor in your program. Evaluations specific to each instructor might provide some value and meaning, but they also open up a world of possibilities for claims of unjust criticism and evaluation. Using the same evaluations for each instructor can also create a self-imposed standard for what the department is looking for in an instructor. Having the whole department work together to co-create an instructor evaluation form can also help encourage buy-in, provide mutually agreed-upon standards, and give instructors a clear sense of what they will be evaluated on. When we know these values, they can inform our own instruction choices.

Instructor evaluations will differ most distinctly from peer observations in that these forms will frequently be filled out by the content professors who were there to observe the class. Students are rarely asked to fill out these forms in part because the information they can offer is often more useful when seen through the lens of a class evaluation, and in practical terms, library faculty and staff members often do not have the time to observe every class. The content professor can fill out the instructor evaluation either immediately after class or later through an online form. Many times, it can help to have a separate location as the drop-off place for these evaluations so that people will feel more comfortable giving honest feedback. On that same note, these evaluations affect people. Receiving feedback on performance frequently feels like a reflection not just on your teaching performance but on you as a person. When delivering this information, watch for signs of discomfort or upset so that you can find ways to subvert negative attitudes toward the evaluation.

"Bad" Assessment Results

The majority of the discussion so far in this chapter has centered on all assessment being a net positive, but there can and will be surprises when we perform assessment because we can find things we were not expecting. How we handle negative results can be just as meaningful as how we handle positive ones. Part of this points toward the meaning of assessment. If all our results met our predictions exactly, the practice of performing the assessment would be almost meaningless. Rather, we are in search of how to improve. So particularly with evaluations, it may be tempting to throw out a result because it does not match what we normally hear about our teaching, but perhaps there is merit to the result. I cannot stress enough that negative results are rarely a personal reflection. It could be poor design of the assessment measurement. Perhaps other ways to measure what you are looking for would yield better results. Or just as likely, sometimes the results are correct but simply reflect poorly on our instruction. For the aware instruction coordinator, bad assessment results should not come as a massive surprise. If anything, they can be used to start a conversation with administration or with the instruction team to find ways to move forward. These numbers will be used as a baseline for establishing and improving results down the road. It can be useful to think of assessment as the foundation for future projects. Don't let negative results impact future work.

Even I struggle to find positivity in negative results. Typically, when my assessments yield results I was not expecting, it seems like a reflection on me as an instructor. Mentally removing myself from the work is a challenge, and from conversations with others, I know I am not alone in this. I can only offer this to you, bad results are only an indicator of where you need to improve. Take time to sit with your results and view them only as they are, not as a reflection on who you are.

Summary

Assessment is the hidden portion of the role of instruction coordinator that many people are not aware of. Constantly making sure that statistics are kept up to date will save you time down the road when generating reports. Make sure you look at past reports or learn from others what style of assessment is preferred by your department.

Worksheets and Activities

Creating an Evaluation Form (Instructor or Classroom)

Use the following questions to guide the process as you go through the experiment:

1. What do we want to learn from this evaluation?
2. What method will help show us what we want to learn?

Figure 6.1 is a great example of a fairly standard instructor evaluation or class observation form that would give specific examples of what to look for and could be evaluated concretely if the data points had been met.

On the flip side, it is so well defined that there is not much room for more open concepts and actions that might not be specifically mentioned within your evaluation. Some evaluations have a more open flow, with only a few specific questions that give room for evaluators to provide personalized feedback. The following is a typical example of that type of form:

1. What was a particularly effective moment during this instruction?
2. What did students gain from this session?
3. Do you have suggestions for future sessions?

Keeping the list of questions short is a practical endeavor, because realistically, most content professors who fill out these forms after the session will

FIGURE 6.1

Class information and instructor statistics
(Date/names/locations, etc.)

Teacher action	Met? (Y/N/NA)	Comments
Defined terms and concepts		
Was able to answer student questions satisfactorily		
Gave time for practice		
Used visuals or handouts		

be in a rush to get to their next classes or meetings, or if they are fill out the form online after the fact, they may well have forgotten the specifics; only highlights and major events will stand out in their memories.

NOTES

1. Peggy L. Maki, "Developing an Assessment Plan to Learn about Student Learning," *Journal of Academic Librarianship* 28, no. 1 (2002): 8–13.
2. ACRL IS Analysis of Instruction Environments Task Force, 2004–2007: Beth S. Woodard (Chair), Barbara Mann, Stephanie Michel, and Terry Taylor, *Analyzing Your Instructional Environment: A Workbook* (Chicago: ACRL, 2010).
3. Lorin W. Anderson and David R. Krathwohl, *A Taxonomy for Learning, Teaching, and Assessing: A Revision of Bloom's Taxonomy of Educational Objectives* (New York: Longman, 2001).
4. Megan Oakleaf, "Are They Learning? Are We? Learning Outcomes and the Academic Library," *Library Quarterly* 81, no. 1 (January 2011): 61–82.

5. Melissa Becher, "Instruction Coordinators and Higher Education Accreditation: A Study of Awareness and Assessment Documentation Use," *Journal of Academic Librarianship* 39, no. 6 (November 2013): 573–81.

6. Joseph R. Matthews, "Assessing Library Contributions to University Outcomes: The Need for Individual Student Level Data," *Library Management* 33, no. 6/7 (September 2012): 389–402.

7. Megan Oakleaf, "Building the Assessment Librarian Guildhall: Criteria and Skills for Quality Assessment," *Journal of Academic Librarianship* 39, no. 2 (March 2013): 126–28.

8. Kyung-Sun Kim and Sei-Ching Joanna Sin, "Use and Evaluation of Information from Social Media in the Academic Context: Analysis of Gap between Students and Librarians," *Journal of Academic Librarianship* 42, no. 1 (2016): 74–82.

9. L. R. Horowitz, "Assessing Library Services: A Practical Guide for the Nonexpert," *Library Leadership and Management* 23 (Fall 2009): 193–203.

10. Rui Wang, "Assessment for One-Shot Library Instruction: A Conceptual Approach," *portal: Libraries and the Academy* 16, no. 3 (2016): 619–48.

11. John F. Chizmar and Anthony L. Ostrosky, "The One-Minute Paper: Some Empirical Findings," *Journal of Economic Education* 29, no. 1 (Winter 1998): 3–10.

12. David J. Turbow and Julie Evener, "Norming a VALUE Rubric to Assess Graduate Information Literacy Skills," *Journal of the Medical Library Association* 104, no. 3 (July 2016): 209–14.

13. Craig A. Mertler, "Designing Scoring Rubrics for Your Classroom," *Practical Assessment, Research and Evaluation* 7, no. 25 (2001): 1–10.

FURTHER READINGS

ACRL IS Analysis of Instruction Environments Task Force, 2004–2007: Beth S. Woodard (Chair), Barbara Mann, Stephanie Michel, and Terry Taylor. *Analyzing Your Instructional Environment: A Workbook.* Chicago: ACRL, 2010.

Anderson, Lorin W., and David R. Krathwohl. *A Taxonomy for Learning, Teaching, and Assessing: A Revision of Bloom's Taxonomy of Educational Objectives.* New York: Longman, 2001.

Becher, Melissa. "Instruction Coordinators and Higher Education Accreditation: A Study of Awareness and Assessment Documentation Use." *Journal of Academic Librarianship* 39, no. 6 (November 2013): 573–81.

Chizmar, John F., and Anthony L. Ostrosky. "The One-Minute Paper: Some Empirical Findings." *Journal of Economic Education* 29, no. 1 (Winter 1998): 3–10.

Horowitz, L. R. "Assessing Library Services a Practical Guide for the Nonexpert." *Library Leadership and Management* 23 (Fall 2009): 193–203.

Kim, Kyung-Sun, and Sei-Ching Joanna Sin. "Use and Evaluation of Information from Social Media in the Academic Context: Analysis of Gap between Students and Librarians." *Journal of Academic Librarianship* 42, no. 1 (2016): 74–82.

Maki, Peggy L. "Developing an Assessment Plan to Learn about Student Learning." *Journal of Academic Librarianship* 28, no. 1 (2002): 8–13.

Matthews, Joseph R. "Assessing Library Contributions to University Outcomes: The Need for Individual Student Level Data." *Library Management* 33, no. 6/7 (September 2012): 389–402.

Mertler, Craig A. "Designing Scoring Rubrics for Your Classroom." *Practical Assessment, Research and Evaluation* 7, no. 25 (2001): 1–10.

Oakleaf, Megan. "Are They Learning? Are We? Learning Outcomes and the Academic Library." *Library Quarterly* 81, no. 1 (January 2011): 61–82.

Oakleaf, Megan. "Building the Assessment Librarian Guildhall: Criteria and Skills for Quality Assessment." *Journal of Academic Librarianship* 39, no. 2 (March 2013): 126–28.

Turbow, David J., and Julie Evener. "Norming a VALUE Rubric to Assess Graduate Information Literacy Skills." *Journal of the Medical Library Association* 104, no. 3 (July 2016): 209–14.

Wang, Rui. "Assessment for One-Shot Library Instruction: A Conceptual Approach." *portal: Libraries and the Academy* 16, no. 3 (2016): 619–48.

Leveraging Technology

Introduction

It is no secret to any currently working librarian that the field has begun to use new technology, rather than the paper-based / analog technology of the past, to enhance the patron experience, often in unseen ways. Ours is a different library than that of the past, and instruction coordinators spend a good deal of time managing technology, from very specific hardware functions to larger issues of figuring out what software is useful for instruction and information literacy and what is ultimately just a flash in the pan. For example, it was only about ten years ago that library classrooms were filled with enthusiastic instructors using clickers to elicit feedback. Now that same technology has shifted once again. Very few instructors still use clickers, and those who did are now using Poll Everywhere or other student-response systems such as Kahoot! that they can easily use with their mobile devices or laptops in the classroom, thereby shifting the burden of supplying and maintaining hardware to the students. For all the negatives that may arise from such practices, usually budgetary reasons are cited for why hardware is often not provided for students. This is fairly typical of many libraries across the nation. There should be no expectation that instructional technology will remain stable, and a large portion of the coordinator's job is to stay on top of trends in technology. This does not mean you will need to be an expert within this subfield, but you will need to know how to make wise decisions for the team, and to keep current on trends that could be used in instruction.

Managing Instructional Tech

Make a mental assessment of the technologies currently used in your library classroom. The obvious things that come to mind are probably physical items, such as desktop computers, laptops, projectors, and possibly microphones and audio systems. These alone are expensive to maintain, operate, and keep up to date. Computer labs are unique in that prospective students and their parents use them in part to judge whether they want to come to the university, because if technology even looks old, then may feel that they will lack the support they need at the university.[1] Instruction coordinators need to keep these things in mind as they request funding and support for the overall functions of the library computer labs, especially if you know these resources can only be updated sparingly or are on a update cycle that is not advantageous to your lab.

Just as hardware is important to the library classroom space, keeping software up to date is also of vital importance, particularly when students will be continuously using the spaces even when library classes are not in session. For example, in late 2015, my computer lab was undergoing renovations, and we decided to be on the leading edge of technology and update all computers to the newly released Windows 10 platform. It seemed like a great idea. Except...students were not used to the platform and had difficulty understanding how to navigate it. IT was still learning about the platform as well and had initial issues managing and providing technological support for it. What seemed like a great idea to get students interested in using the space actually turned into a major source of time and frustration, and instructors had to spend extra time before and after class explaining the basics.

Web-based applications are often great free resources for librarians to use for a particular lesson plan and instruction, but the support for them is often lacking due to the lack of financial incentive on their part. Sometimes these applications were created years ago and are no longer supported, so you might need to remind students that the program can only be used in one particular browser or with specialized features turned off. These things take small amounts of time here and there, but it adds up. The ideal lesson plan would account for small errors and accommodations that take place when problems arise, but realistically, many lesson plans have little wiggle room to begin with. The fifty minutes of class time is precious, and many instructors seek to preserve that by sticking to a format that they know will work.

When Technology Fails

Realistically, if the internet goes down or power goes out during a class, the best option is almost always going to be to cancel class and reschedule. But how should you handle smaller issues, like when an application is not working perfectly or a few computer stations are having issues?

- Always have a backup plan for the technology (another way for the lesson to be demonstrated or taught).
- Ask that people pair up if a program is failing on just a few devices.
- Ask one or two students to demonstrate for the class rather than having the entire class do so (preferably on the instructor's station for all to see).
- Be willing and able to reschedule the class for a future date when the technology is functioning.
- Have class discussion options in mind.
- Have self-guided worksheets available that they can take home and do at a later time.

In addition to making sure that students can capably use software and hardware, the instruction coordinator needs to make sure that the instructors who regularly use the space feel comfortable using it. If instructors are uncomfortable using a technology for whatever reason, they simply will not use it. While from a practical standpoint, that may make sense to them, from the library's perspective, a great deal of money has been invested in this technology, and no one is using it. If instructors cannot teach students to use the technology, who will ultimately be able to use it? Issues like this can make it hard for administrators to justify purchasing more technology down the road. Taking preventative measures by training the instructors well beforehand and making sure that they are comfortable using the technology on their own can help. Referring back to the concept of observation, one small step toward building comfort is to be the other person in the room when an instructor tries out a new technology. Another way is to have a group "playdate" where everyone gets a chance to try out the new technology. This can help create a sense of comfort so that should something fail, another person knows how to resolve the situation. When technology fails in the middle of a lesson, it can be deeply distressing, especially if the lesson plan relies heavily upon it. Having backup plans even if the problem never occurs can help ease these moments. When panic sets into instruction, learning walks out the door. If a technology fails, take a deep breath, close your eyes and remember your objectives and go back to the basics of what you know to do. For the instruction coordinator, this can sometimes create a thorny relationship issue, and the coordinator will have to do a lot of explaining to professors. On these rare occasions, professors who took time out of their scheduled syllabus and course meetings for their students to learn specific skills might voice their frustrations. These semester classes can be so filled with goals to meet in just sixteen weeks that there is not enough filler time for ancillary options such as going to a library class that fails and hoping the next opportunity will work instead. By that point next week, or even at the next session, the professor may have moved on to an entirely new subject area, or students may have already turned in their papers. The instruction coordinator should reinforce the need for information literacy and offer solutions that can meet the needs of students and professors. Some options include having students come to the office one-on-one or in pairs to learn on their own, offering the class at a different time that may potentially be shorter, or even allowing the professor to have time at the beginning or end of class to teach the vital issues that still need to be covered.

Although not all of these fixes will be able to accommodate everything, the instruction coordinator acts as the go-between for the instruction librarian and the professor, especially during sticky situations where an outside voice can be appreciated by all sides. For the instruction librarian, it can be calming to have another person in his or her corner who understands the issues, particularly if it involves library technologies that are hard to discuss with others. Of course, finding the line between what is bullying behavior and what is not can often require a gut-level understanding. Many professors are willing to understand that technology errors happen from time to time, but not always. The role of instruction coordinator is not simply a passive one built to assuage unhappy patrons; it is structured to advocate for librarians and make sure that their best interests are served. Speaking up in library roles can sometimes be difficult, especially as "making changes that don't benefit those in power can be difficult, even when those in power claim to want to reach related goals."[2]

Tech support is generally available to help with the harder maintenance issues, especially those that involve hardware, but it is up to the instruction coordinator to be aware of the computer lab's low-level needs, such as when a piece of hardware is not working, and follow up with the appropriate resources. Understanding basic technology issues can help people determine what can be easily fixed on the spot and what will require backup. Easy fixes include items such as loose cables, which can make it appear as if audio systems or monitors are not working, or aspect ratios that may have been switched. Knowing who to contact for this type of support might rely on institutional memory not easily passed on to new hires. Creating a prominently displayed contact list can help instructors who use the space intermittently, particularly as this information is not always known from group to group. Even if your own library instructors know who to contact, if there are ever visiting professors or classes led by someone other than a librarian, they may not necessarily know who to contact. In these instances, it may be worth creating a standard operating procedure (SOP) for your position or, if one has already been created, having contacts included in it for both you and others to refer back to. SOPs are useful for routine interactions and jobs that can be performed by anyone in the position, and these items, while rare in the library world, can help formalize a repeated process that might feel nebulous in the beginning.

Many libraries are trending toward allowing other groups to use their instruction labs when the library is not already scheduled in them, particularly for group meetings and demonstrations that require computers. As these situations increase, the need for someone to be on hand for backup becomes more necessary. In that scenario, the instruction coordinator is usually the

first person called in the rapid-fire chain to get help. In addition to a prominently displayed contact list, preferably next to a phone, it is worth keeping
a list of known issues and notes for anyone who may be new to the setup. In
some cases, if time is available, it is worth meeting with the leaders of these
events to go over the setup details for the room in advance. In this way, they
will not likely need to contact you unless it is for an uncommon aberration,
which in most cases could not be prepared for regardless. These small details
add up, and working to create a welcoming and easy-to-use space on the first
try can be helpful when each lab across campus may have its own unique
quirks. Starting at a very basic level by labeling buttons and giving the order
of operations with buttons can help anyone use the classroom with mini-
mal help from you or others. As mentioned, when we installed Windows 10
onto the computer lab machines, even some professors had difficulty using
them. Icons and logos needed identification. Even in the transfer from PC to
Mac, people can be somewhat confused. This is not an issue unique to just
professors. Although frequently labeled as digital natives, students can also
be confused when confronted with technologies that they do not regularly
use. Technology is pervasive, but that does not mean that everyone inherently understands the most up-to-date versions. Issues like this are quiet.
People may not let you know when they do not understand a technology, and
it may seem like setting up preventative measures for rarities like this are
meaningless or take up too much time, but it is precisely because they are so
rare that they are worth doing. Writing down basic details and processes can
help those who are newer to the system as well as those who may not be as
involved with instruction as the coordinator is.

Also keep in mind that not all instructors use the same technology at
the same times, so they may encounter issues that others would not. In some
cases, these issues vary based on how the technology is being used (such as
trying to access a database with a limited number of seats), or they could be
based on outside issues (such as routine maintenance that happens only in
the evenings). Perhaps an issue only arises in mornings after the program
loads for the first time, or maybe the problem only occurs when two or more
specific programs run simultaneously. Documenting these issues is vital to
getting help and figuring out how to fix problems. If, as instruction coordinator, you are the chief one doing repairs, keep these issues in the back of your
mind. Make sure that instructors have a systematic way to let you and others
know about issues before they steamroll into a larger problem that could have

Sample Emergency Contact Form

Need Help?

For room maintenance issues: Call [instruction coordinator] at x5555.
For computer issues: Call [Information Technology] at x5555.
To turn ON the projector:

- Press the Power button on the panel insert in the podium.
- The projector will take sixty seconds to warm up.

To turn OFF the projector:

- Push the Power button on the panel insert in the podium, then push again when "Power Off?" message appears on the screen.
- The projector will take ninety seconds to cool down.

easily been fixed earlier on. Such a system can be tricky to implement, if only because we all have busy schedules, and trying to catch individuals during the busy instruction season is not always the easiest thing. When there are back-to-back classes, certainly, grab the next instructor on the way in and let him or her know about screens that are not working or databases that appear to be down. But what about when the issues appear at the end of the day or when a class is not scheduled immediately afterward? Some solutions are group chat programs like Slack or Skype for Business, in which all members of the instruction team can be added and have an area to post questions about classes and prepping and, yes, to alert others to known issues in the lab. Ideal solutions to these scenarios tend to be highly individualistic and unique to departments. They also depend on how information tends to migrate in an institution. Sometimes it goes back and forth, and in some situations, people do not automatically think to alert others. The solution relies on understanding your organizational culture, which can be changed slowly over time but usually will take the effort of more than one person.

Sourcing

Finding good technology is a hassle. With the exception of technology purchases driven by the administration, many times the choice of what will be used in the classroom is driven by the instruction coordinator. This is a gift not to be overlooked, but at the same time, determining which technologies to bring into the classroom can be confusing at best. Many technologies look interesting before a demo; sometimes once you see the demo, it is nothing new. New technologies are introduced at a seemingly nonstop rate. This is an area where the size of your institution will affect many of the decisions you make or are capable of making. Instruction coordinators rarely have final say on the purchase of a large technological purchase like a Learning Management System (LMS) such as Blackboard, Canvas or D2L, but they can offer advice to the main drivers on campus who are seeking input. Better-funded universities tend to have technology initiatives and support staff who can help maintain the software and hardware on campus, whereas colleges and universities with smaller budgets may not have a dedicated IT person for the library or the funds to invest in new technologies and updates every year. To be on the forefront of new technologies draws students in but also takes a good deal of manpower and support. The coordinator needs to be on the look-out for technologies that will (1) help students and (2) mirror and enhance the way instructors are teaching. These two things combined will help push your instructors toward using the technology and, most desired, further the educational outcomes of students. It is easy to say that since your university is smaller or lacks support that initiatives cannot happen at your institution. However, talking to other institutions about how they brought specific technologies to campus and what the onboarding process was like, as well as the continuing support issues, can help give you a better sense of what is needed on your part to make sure that a technology will be effective. In a few cases, due to either cost or manpower, a smaller institution truly cannot bring something on, and in others, it is possible with resource sharing and figuring out who in your system can help support you.

Keep in mind how students currently use technology. You can casually observe use as you walk around campus, but other more specific information can be garnered by speaking to specific departments on campus or through comprehensive surveys. One frequently overlooked population group when considering technology needs is distant and online students. Even if the instruction team is only involved with these groups through a learning management system (LMS), you can find technologies to accommodate users who primarily see the university through an internet browser and may only come to campus for graduation at most. Figuring out how new technologies will affect these users before they are implemented will greatly improve their experience with the library. For them making efficient use of LibGuides specific to online students or thinking of how they navigate our resources, can be extremely helpful. The specifics of technology can be intimidating to some people, especially when they feel that they do not understand new terms and uses that accompany them, but you can circumvent this when purchasing new technologies by asking questions about use. Asking obvious questions may seem silly at first, but these inroads lead to the nitty-gritty details and terms that you can press for further information on. Also, a few purchasing guides can be found at tech websites like Gizmodo and others, and user reviews will give you a specific understanding of what to expect. It is also worth checking to see if the institution has a house purchasing guide you can employ in these situations. For some library products, particularly those offered through major vendors such as ProQuest and EBSCO, the only chance a library has to get direct experience with a product is through onsite demonstrations or at conferences. Each of these options has downsides, such as time and expense, and finding libraries that are already using the technology in the real world can provide an invaluable day-to-day perspective for how a product is used in the field.

Conferences, posters, and presentations are all great ways to learn about technologies currently used by other institutions. Sometimes you'll learn about a new product and how it is helping instructors tremendously, or in other cases, you'll learn about a technology that is not helpful and will be warned against using it in the future. The conference back-channels mentioned earlier in the book can be useful to find out specifics on a particular technology. People who attended the same sessions as you may have used the technologies and had different experiences or simply want to voice their assent that it is a great product. These backchannels also frequently highlight issues that the vendors themselves might be hesitant to bring up themselves. Although these unofficial channels can be difficult to vet, they can help give credence to the information you have already gathered.

Many universities and colleges have preapproved contracts with vendors so that all specific technology items will come from a few select sources. Sometimes this can be very limiting for an instruction coordinator, and in other cases, it encourages creativity, especially in finding outside grants that may fund the purchase of specialized technologies. On the flip side, when there are preapproved contracts with specific vendors, some libraries can get special discounts on technologies they otherwise would not be able to afford.

It is a complex dance, and it is vital for an instruction coordinator to have a budget in hand while making these decisions and to be aware of the library's strategic plan. Even if it is not money that you can spend directly through a company credit card or invoice, having an idea of how much can be spent on new technologies gives you a firm grasp of the parameters and scope of technology you can request.

When I was first pricing new computers for my lab, I found the process to be mysterious because I did not have a firm budget. I could request items, but sometimes they would be mysteriously denied, or only certain parts would be allowed. Simple details could have vastly changed the look and feel of the computer lab. Today I am pleased with how it looks and operates, but I would change certain things if I could do it over again, technology being a central part of that. Most large-scale projects will have issues you wish you could go back and change, but if you have a list of essentials that must be in place by the end of the project, this will give you a better sense of what was truly necessary for function and what would just have been nice to have.

Check It Out!

Straying outside your professional comfort zone can introduce you to others working on similar topics that may help you. Some other professional organizations work on technology and access issues too. NASIG (formerly the North American Serials Interest Group, Inc.) can be a great resource for librarians looking for information on vendor negotiations and electronic resources. **www.nasig.org**

For smaller programs with fewer people on staff, it is not unheard of to have to perform some basic technical support for the items in the lab. In this case, during the sourcing portion of acquisition, it can be incredibly helpful to read reviews on technology forums such as NewEgg or ALA TechSource (which focuses less on specific reviews than on applications of technology). Most major library products have listservs and toolboxes that can help as well. Amazon's reviews have become less reliable for technology, and it recommended that these be considered as many information literacy directives are issued. The amount of support you can give to technological issues may be limited, but you can fix common issues before they become larger ones. Knowing your technical limits can be useful in judging not only when to call in help but also what types of research areas you may be lacking and how you can start strengthening them through outside training.

Types of Technology

Many of the websites, applications, and software available for educational use are initially offered for free or low cost only to later have (more) costs tacked on. A common term for this is freemium resources, in which the service is offered on a multitiered system, with the base level being free but the more useful features hidden behind paywalls and subscription services. There are a few different ways to approach using these sources, especially as many lack an educational user agreement allowing multiple users licenses. Many of the services available through these products cannot be easily replicated, and if you decide to use them, it may be worth having a conversation about access rights and how much information to give to a company, particularly about what happens to the user information. Once you start these conversations, students may want to know why the lesson is proceeding with a freemium resource, so it is worthwhile to have a public statement available for your justifications. Making blanket decisions to use or not use these resources can be frustrating, because so many web resources that target student learning have these particular issues.

A great example is the graphic design site Canva, which allows students to create their own posters, presentations, and social media–oriented infographics. Using this site can be helpful to students wanting to create pieces with a professional look, but the downside is that many of the elements necessary to create that professional look have a price to them. Though each element, such as a particular font or a nice photograph or frame, is usually only a dollar, these items quickly add up. The prices are not always prominently displayed either. The price can be a "surprise" when you go to purchase, and for some students, it may well be an unwelcome surprise. When these problems are considered together, it becomes troublesome to justify a source, no matter how good, to students who realistically may not have the financial literacy or the simple cash to spend on a school project. Complicating the issue is that this tool is very dominant at the moment for several fields, such as public relations and media production. Students want to use it, but it is hard to rationalize. Identifying how to present information to students that is complicated is hard for instructors to do. In these circumstances, it is worth it for the instruction coordinator to be aware of not only what products are vital to specific fields but how to navigate the issues associated with them. Obviously, it is impractical for an instruction coordinator to be aware of every product and piece of software used by every department and major at the university, not to mention the complications and issues related to these products. Still, as you become aware of them, file them away in a system useable by you and others so that the list can be amended and edited in the future. Complete mastery of these subjects is not expected, but it is helpful to listen to frustrations and see where a librarian can jump in and help.

Technology Update Cheat Sheet

- ability to export data in a standardized format
- information can be secured from outside sources
- can be used on a mobile interface
- site access is ADA compliant

Mobile applications, apps for short, are also increasingly an option built into information literacy and educational settings. Smartphones are prevalent in the lives of most students, and it is natural to want to reach out to them where they already are. Likely, your students have already brought their devices into your classroom, so taking advantage of them can help leverage their attention toward the instruction quite literally at hand. Your library webpage may have its own app for class demonstrations, particularly for functions involving searching the catalog or the "ask a librarian" feature, but these are usually more akin to a website demonstration than actual information literacy. Databases have some mobile access, but it is hit or miss as to which ones do. The trouble with mobile apps is that students usually do not want to download and use an app on their phones or tablets unless absolutely necessary. They might have limited storage on their devices or simply see it as a hassle to add apps just because a teacher says so. Mobile applications can operate like freemium sources; when downloaded, some apps ask for permission to use the contents of the device, and students may not feel comfortable providing access. Apps with more of an information literacy bent are those that can be used beyond the library classroom, such as Evernote or hypothes.is for annotation. The catch is to make sure that any application taught in class has a direct tie-in to an information literacy component. Using apps just because they are new and flashy will not ultimately help students learn how to discern and use technology. Prepping for these classes will also involve a great amount of upfront work on the instructor's part to make sure that all devices can use the app (some are only iOS compliant, or some may not be supported on outdated devices). And the instructor will need to thoroughly map out how the app will be used in class, step by step, so that any unexpected technology issues can be minimized in advance. These are all doable things, and the instruction coordinator's role is to potentially remind instructors about the setup needed and ask how they plan on tying the information together. Even offering to partner or aid in a complicated project can be a great help.

When iPhones and other smartphones were new to the technology scene, being aware of cost and who did and did not have them could be limiting factors for lesson plans. When I first began teaching in the library around 2007, one could not assume that most students would have smartphones. These items were not commonplace, and to build a lesson around the use of the devices would have been absurd. As these items become closer to staples for personal electronics, it is worth being aware that not all students have a smartphone to use, and you should have backup pans in place that include either partnering or applications that can be accessed via a web presence. Keep this general idea in mind for most new technologies with the assumption that while people may be excited about new technologies, they may not always have them at hand or be fluent in using them.

All of these technologies, but perhaps most pressing for apps is to remind students to think critically about their digital world and how they are impacted by the algorithms that present them information on not just a daily basis, but in some cases a constant basis. There are no standardized competencies for understanding digital literacy, but many of the Frames for Information Literacy can pair well with the practice. Help your students to question the information that comes to them through these interfaces.

Currently, a host of technologies are employed by libraries that focus on **assessment of skills.** These technologies are varied but focus on testing students on a set of predetermined skills, such as comprehension of site navigation and the location of information. Examples include Sidecar Learning, sprung from University of Arizona's Guide on the Side and Educational Testing Service's iSkills. Many corporate offerings have a slicker feel than the homegrown options hosted on various LibGuides, but the questions are often lacking in specific areas that an information literacy program might have tailored to a specific department or group. The tradeoff is that your department does not need to hire or use the time of someone in the IT department to build the assessment tools for you. Factoring in human labor costs, purchasing these options can seem much cheaper in the long run. These products are best used to get a sense of where students are as well as to give instructors a sense of where to begin their instruction. They can also be used independent of one-shot instruction classes so that students can teach themselves library skills without needing an instructor to guide them through the basics. These options are great for students who might need some extra time catching up to the rest of their class or need a refresher after time away from the library or university.

Another area of note for instruction are **cloud-based services**—those not locally hosted on library machines but kept in a system of offsite servers, such as Amazon's S3 and DuraFront. Many parts of library services, such as catalog records and student records, are slowly shifting to these cloud services, but be aware if your students will be creating documents with sensitive information that they may not want to share. The likelihood of using cloud-based services when interacting with instruction software is very high, as the costs for the patron can be differed and the products can be accessed from multiple devices. If you are not sure if you are using a cloud-based service, look at some of your favorite online services and read their terms more carefully; you may be surprised. One of the most popular services for use with education is Dropbox. This platform allows a person to share and access files across multiple devices, all of them synced up to the most current version. For class assignments, this can be invaluable to the instructor, especially in a multiple-session class in which students may need to partner with other students.

Offered through some paid services and some freemium services, **screencasting** has played a role in instruction for those who wish to share the specifics of what they are doing on screen with others. Jing is one of the most commonly used in libraries for virtual reference, though not as frequently used with instruction. ScreenFlow and CamStudio are also common examples of screencasting services that can be used by instructors. These services are particularly good for instruction for off-campus and online students who still need to know how to use services but frequently need a visual approach toward grasping specific concepts. There are even a few services that allow one user to remotely take over the desktop of another to help with more complex subjects. Although these applications are typically used by IT personnel helping to troubleshoot issues that they may be able to more readily see, there are areas in instruction where they may be useful, especially if patrons have very specific problems librarians could quickly help them with.

Some popular instructional technologies

- Jing
- Piktochart
- Dropbox
- Google Documents
- Padlet

Quick Recap

Types of sources can include freemium resources, mobile applications, skills assessment, cloud-based services, and screencasting. Specific products vary and can sometimes be covered by more than one of these broad categories.

Promoting Library Technologies

In a book on library instruction, it would be remiss not to mention the many technological innovations housed within the library walls that students will need to learn to use. Though they vary by institution, increasingly the collections held within a library deviate from traditional resources students may associate with the word *library*. Instruction librarians are the best resources to promote these new technologies and tools to users who would otherwise be unaware. Instruction focusing solely on database demonstrations and library tours is certainly necessary at times, but focusing on different areas of the library can make for a more well-rounded experience for the student. Some of these locations can be with building partners such as an office of Disability Services or perhaps Academic Advising. This is a clear area where partnerships and a full understanding of what the library has to offer can be invaluable. Both as a way for the individual units to work in cohesion, but also for the instruction coordinator to learn what services these other units may have to offer that are instruction related.

Knowing how things such as **institutional repositories (IR)** that contain local collections or even specific software like survey tools hosted through the library (Qualtrics, SurveyMonkey, etc.) can be used and leveraged by faculty members is vital to promoting them. It is tempting to think of these things as high-level tools, but they can actually be as simple as things like

interlibrary loan (ILL). If the instruction librarian only has a baseline understanding of how a product works, providing information to potential users
not only can be hard for the librarian but may fail to hook users who do
not fully understand why the product works. Comprehension is the first step
toward better promotion. The more the instruction librarian understands the
value and importance of the product, the better they can promote it by knowing who would be able to make the best use out of it and how to troubleshoot
problems or stress points that might confuse new users or turn them away
from future use. The obvious rejoinder to this is that our time is limited and
learning every software package and product that the library offers would be
burdensome and unrealistic. This is true. More realistically, librarians, and
especially instruction librarians, have areas they are assigned to or work most
frequently with. Think, for example, of an instruction librarian who works
almost exclusively with music and theater departments. In his or her case,
it would not be worth the time to learn the specifics of engineering and science packages (though they probably shouldn't be unaware of them), but it
would be vital to understand software directed toward music production or
set design. Getting to know your faculty, particularly their research areas, can
also give you a better understanding of whether they are open to learning
new technologies or happy with the products they have been using. All of
these things factor into good promotion techniques.

Related to good promotion is knowing the timing for and practicalities
of introducing patrons to new technology. This can be a very careful dance.
Too much too soon, and they can become overwhelmed, and too little information on your part, and they will lack desire to learn more. Know your
own limits, including how well you understand a product and how well
enmeshed you are in a department. If a product is not going to work particularly well for a faculty member, let him or her know. Do not build up a
product to be something it is not. Other options include creating a **marketing
plan** that can easily be adapted to unique situations across campus but still
manages to address the needs of your patron group. These plans generally
include the target audience, purpose, goals, and methods. Although it may
seem silly to create a marketing plan for a specific department or even group
of faculty members, it can be helpful to have a script to rely on with specific
checkpoints built in to keep librarians accountable and help them know that
they are on target.

What's a Marketing Plan?

These items can be developed in house to reflect how marketing materials and projects will be deployed. Sometimes they can include action items that get detailed or they can include who is in charge of specific tasks and the timelines for how these actions will be accomplished.

A key task that can help with promotion but does not feel overwhelming to both librarians and the faculty who are targeted is to send specific updates on new technologies as they appear. So knowing that certain faculty members may be exclusively using one product, a librarian can let them know when new updates appear and offer to do one-on-one instruction to get them up to speed or even target a specific class that is using the product so that everyone can learn en masse. Promotion and marketing can feel massive, but when broken down into approachable parts, the instruction coordinator can keep track of where each of these notions are stationed at.

LibGuides and research guides are frequently created to allow students and faculty to read and parse information on their own time and as a reference that can be referred back to outside of the classroom. As their use has grown to encompass a larger share of libraries, they have also come to be used for broader concepts beyond their original subject guide frames. Instruction coordinators can look to these for specific technology guides that can be easily updated and pointed to for faculty who want to do things on their own. Creating materials like guides is part of the often hidden work of an instruction librarian. The coordinator needs to know what areas of these guides should be developed, and critically, not all guides need to last forever. Digital weeding needs to take place for some guides created with a specific purpose or class in mind but that will no longer be needed for future use.[3] Digital weeding may sound overwhelming, especially considering that individual webpages can amass quickly, but it can be as simple as hiding the pages and URLs from direct public view or deleting the whole guide. Going through this process, it is important to look at use statistics such as view counts and downloads and to be aware of what classes are currently being taught and how actively other groups are using the guides. In some cases, even if a class is no longer being taught, the department may have memory of the site and be using it quite frequently. An example of this is when I created a guide for the writing center on the Scholarship of Teaching and Learning (SOTL). This guide was for a specific project of one semester and I worked in tangent with the professor in creating it. I did not unpublish it after that semester ended, but I did not update it either. It was only in 2019, 4 years after I had first created the guide that I found out that professor was still using the guide in his classes. I only learned of this when he complained about a broken link.

This type of analytic information is relatively easy to gather through Lib-Guides, but if you are using another system for your research guides, the same information can be gathered through Google Analytics and other tools. If you have administrator privileges within these systems, this work may be done relatively quickly.

LibGuides have changed the library scene in terms of how instruction materials are presented. These items can be changed rapidly to reflect the current scene or specific classes and attitudes. They also create a similar issue that is often warned against regarding Wikipedia. Although many teachers and librarians have learned to better explain how to effectively use Wikipedia, the general refrain ten years ago was that this information could be changed by anyone repeatedly, so the page visited on Monday might be different from the one on Tuesday. So if we are presenting LibGuides as reputable sources to our students, students who have bookmarked LibGuides or are repeatedly visiting one for each paper or project that they work on could find it disconcerting when information has disappeared or changed drastically from what they remember. This internal hypocrisy creates a conflict about how to deal with these materials and our students, and at minimum, we must be aware of these conflicts in order to give our students a better perspective on the fallibility of information professionals just as others.

Selecting which classes to target and how to teach these products in class can be filled with challenges and rewards. It is easy to lean toward a demonstration model of these types of resources, but consider other ways of teaching beyond lectures. Design a class activity that gets students to use these products in ways that encourage them to create or discover discreet objects that target their specific learning needs, perhaps by finding a primary source through the IR or getting a scholarly article through ILL. When students leave class with objects that directly help them with their research and learning, these are the classes that are most rewarding to them. When all your classes are meeting these targets, the role of promoting new technologies can be self-fulfilling.

Conclusion

Technology functions best in the classroom as an aid that guides the peda-gogical practices we have always been following. The downfall is that tech-nology does not always work in the ways that we are expecting, and when it fails, it can wreck an entire lesson plan in seconds. Learning how to sub-vert the failures and live with them when they happen are critical to having a happy relationship with technology in your instruction space. Coordina-tors can guide the conversation on how technology influences our students and faculty as well as promote resources to assist those librarians with less face-to-face time with students. The nature of technology, especially at an academic institution, is to expect change. Coordinators cannot dictate instruction methods or even materials that will stay stable or static, but they can build institutional ways of keeping abreast of the literature and current technologies without getting overwhelmed.

NOTES

1. David Brown and Barbara Sen, "The Undergraduate Prospectus as a Marketing Tool for Academic Libraries," *New Review of Academic Librarianship* 16, no. 2 (2010): 160–91.
2. Jessica Schomberg and Kirsti Cole, "Hush…: The Dangers of Silence in Academic Libraries," In the *Library with the Lead Pipe* (blog), 2016.
3. Mike Waugh, Michelle Donlin, and Stephanie Braunstein, "Next-Generation Collection Management: A Case Study of Quality Control and Weeding E-books in an Academic Library," *Collection Management* 40, no. 1 (2015): 17–26.

FURTHER READINGS

Brown, David, and Barbara Sen. "The Undergraduate Prospectus as a Marketing Tool for Academic Libraries." *New Review of Academic Librarianship* 16, no. 2 (2010): 160–91.

Schomberg, Jessica, and Kirsti Cole. "Hush…: The Dangers of Silence in Academic Libraries." In the *Library with the Lead Pipe* (blog). 2016.

Waugh, Mike, Michelle Donlin, and Stephanie Braunstein. "Next-Generation Collection Management: A Case Study of Quality Control and Weeding E-books in an Academic Library." *Collection Management* 40, no. 1 (2015): 17–26.

8

Best Practices

Introduction

In this chapter, I draw from my survey and interviews with instruction coordinators. I was struck by both the differences and the similarities of the roles created by those who worked in completely different institutions. Sometimes things like our own personal fears or insecurities shine through, particularly in the section dealing with education, in which some people discussed how they felt they did not take enough or the "right" classes to perform the role. While it could be worth reflecting on what sparks these thoughts, the important thing to remember is that they are all doing the job—and amazingly so. In this chapter, there are stories of librarians helping their students and the librarians they work with in unique and amazing ways. Consider reading this chapter with a sense of how you interact with others, and reflect on how you can bring similar methods into your own practice.

Who Is a Coordinator?

As I began this project, it was easy to come up with preconceptions of instruction coordinators. Just as librarians in general are always battling stereotypes of who a librarian is (female, elderly, cardigan-wearing, etc.), as I began to see responses from librarians across the United States, it was surprising who instruction coordinators actually were. Apparently, a lot of us are! My own preconceptions were challenged, even though I have filled the role myself and have known several others. I got responses from new coordinators just as frequently as librarians who were no longer coordinators but had opinions, and there were those who lacked the official title but filled in the duties with admirable skill. Spoiler alert: most people who responded to the survey were not elderly women in cardigans!

The gender breakdown, unsurprisingly, fell along lines similar to the profession as a whole. What surprised me were my own biases of how long people stayed within the role and how many years of experience each had. I had assumed that this role was often for people with some experience and that in general, people did not stay in the role for long. I was proven very wrong on this front. Some people had worked in the role for a short time, but many had been in the role for more than ten years!

While many who replied were new to their positions, far more had stayed in their roles for many years and had little or no plan to change that. Although many factors can keep a person in the same role long term, many instruction coordinators were happy with their roles. For those in the first years of the role, the future is still unfolding. When I talked with these coordinators, many felt that they were still learning, but once I delved into their experiences, the experiences and decisions mirrored those of the coordinators who had been in the role for a longer time—especially those experiences focused on scheduling and departmental conflicts.

TABLE 8.1

Instruction coordination by institution type

K–12	1
Community college	6
College/university	23
Research university	11
Liberal arts university	4
Specialized	1
Other	0

TABLE 8.2

Length of time in role

0–3	20
4–6	11
7–10	8
More than 10 years	5

Retrospective Learning

An incredibly common theme was the fact that professors tend to be trained as specialists within their specific fields, and little educational focus is given to actually teaching effectively.[1] Librarian instructors are not immune to this trend either. When asked to look at the roles they were currently filling versus the roles they believed they would be filling when in library and graduate school, many instruction coordinators reflected on the aspects of the role that they had not realized would be as prevalent. The responses ran the gamut: An older librarian wished she had had the opportunity to take a speech class and get fully comfortable speaking in front of varied groups. Others stressed that they had no idea of the amount of assessment work they would be asked to do and wished that they had taken the opportunity to learn more about statistics and assessment design. One of the more common refrains was for an increased focus on pedagogy. Many did not start their careers with any formalized training on how to teach or the basics of educational design. Instead, many came from varied backgrounds and felt they spent the early years of their time as coordinators and instruction librarians learning the fundamentals of pedagogy. Universities, having become aware of this situation, frequently create SOTL centers or offices to help train their professors after the fact. Instruction coordinators who do not have access to an SOTL-type program at their universities might want to do some background reading on the area in order to inform themselves and potentially the librarians who teach with them. If you do have access to an SOTL program, get to know the director and those who have buy-in to the program. Frequently, these faculty learning communities are filled with the types of professors who are most engaged with their classrooms. As a result, they are frequently interested in bringing information literacy components into their classrooms and lessons. Outreach frequently happens in organic ways, and it is rare to find a group of educators so receptive to information literacy.

Real Talk: Not Everyone Finds Pedagogy Fun

"Even though I love instruction and am immersed in that world, my colleagues may not be. Finding ways to make the exciting bits of pedagogy interesting to others and have them see the relevance is a bigger part of the job than I anticipated (and at times more of a challenge)." —Carolyn Gardner, California State University, Dominguez Hills

Many cited that going to Association of College and Research Libraries' (ACRL's) Immersion gave them a greater understanding of how to teach information literacy in a more nuanced manner. The Immersion course has multiple tracks, each focused on different areas of librarianship. While no particular track was cited more than any other, natural areas for an instruction coordinator to consider would be the teacher track or the program track. Each offers weeklong intensive courses that focus either on the teacher as an individual or on an instruction program as a whole. These immersive courses show the institution's commitment to the work of instruction and the coordinators themselves. Attendees learn discrete skills that can be directly applied to the instruction program. A university driven program that has a smaller cohort, but similar praise is Dartmouth University's Librarians Active Learning Institute. This institute is also notable in that it embraces not just instruction librarians, but archivists and special collections librarians as well, basically any librarian with teaching responsibilities. Another ALA-sponsored training program that many have found useful is the ALA Leadership Institute. As opposed to Immersion, the Leadership Institute focuses more closely on midcareer librarians who are primed to transition into a leadership role. Not all instruction coordinators do this, but those who do may also be chairs or leaders of a larger department, and they find the techniques in this weeklong course to be useful for them. In particular, the Leadership Institute can help newer supervisors and administrators who have not yet had the chance to fully form or explore leadership theories and techniques. Another option that may help new coordinators looking to understand their leadership strengths when they cannot take time to go to Immersion or even the Leadership Institute is to look into using the Gallup StrengthsQuest that focuses on academia and education to figure out how leaders can find and manipulate their strengths. Unlike the programs that take coordinators away from their work, this program is available for relatively cheap online. As travel budgets stretch, it becomes important to prioritize where funds are applied, and if training can be done without expensive travel, it is worth it.

How Do I Get into Immersion?

A good application for Immersion involves letters of support from your dean or supervisor, a letter from another reference, and a carefully written essay about your views on instruction.

Be sure to apply to a track that is right for you at your point in librarianship. Some tracks are more advanced than others and have prerequirements. While others are better for the new librarian.

Many coordinators felt that although they wanted to continue learning and engaging with the profession, they were so busy performing their jobs that they did not have the time to continue their education. New models were pushed to the backburner unless something forced the issue to make them work for more. Many chose to attend only one or two conferences a year, specifically those that were not during instruction time, and focus on shorter webinars that were more focused on specific areas that they wanted to work on. Of particular interest were webinars sponsored by an instruction organization such as LIRT (Library Instruction Round Table) or even larger institutions such as ACRL or LLAMA (Library Leadership and Management Association). These groups tend to offer webinars and short courses targeted at instruction coordinators more frequently or at minimum offer ideas that they can sow with the librarians they work with. Some librarians found that their other commitments frequently got in the way of watching the webinar in real time, but because recordings are often sent to attendees after the fact, they could then watch the webinar at their own speed when they had free time.

Traditionally, research libraries have kept fairly strong collections on library science theory and practice. These resources can be invaluable for finding ideas and understanding tasks the coordinator may face, especially since keeping abreast of the field literature helps instructors and coordinators learn best practices and techniques. However, some of these collections are growing smaller through weeding, electronic collections, and the need for space. Survey the scope of your current library science collection, and see how much of it is dedicated to library instruction. Although some resources may be dated, a few have stood the test of time and can prove to be continually useful. For example, the Library Cookbook series has incredibly practical advice that many librarians still use despite its having been published in 2009. Some coordinators have had success with hosting a team "journal club" focusing solely on information literacy and pedagogy.

These journal clubs can often expose you and your teammates to ideas you might not have considered before, but even if none of the ideas comes to fruition, the act of thinking about theory and outside methods of teaching can encourage people to bring new ideas to the table. This gives you, the instruction coordinator, the added bonus of enabling instructors to work on projects that interest them rather than simply proceeding with a top-down approach of dictating what all instructors should focus on.

Tips for a Successful Journal Club

- Give everyone time to read the article before the meeting, but have additional copies on hand in case others have not had the time to read the article.
- Although you do not need to use the same set of questions to examine an article each time, it is nice to come prepared with prompts for attendees, such as the following: How was the research conducted? Would this method be useful in our library?
- Consider making recordings or notes for those who were unable to attend.
- As Zoom has become more widely known, it's easier than ever to bring in a guest lecturer to discuss their article that you have all read in advance.
- Allow for group participation. Rather than being the sole selector of articles, allow your teammates to alternate article selection. A bonus is that this will give you insight into the areas that interest them.

Frequently, research libraries have extensive collections designed to allow both students and faculty to do their own research as opposed to libraries with collections focused more on the content being taught and less on exploratory research. With large student populations comes a higher number of classes and a more varied range of content. One of the most common points of reference from coordinators from every type of institution, but especially from research institutions, was that this is a highly relational role. Instruction coordinators must rely on their people skills to maintain and create relationships with professors and others at all levels of the university. One coordinator at a large research university wrote about having to routinely teach for a professor she did not like on a personal level, but because the classes needed to be taught, she had to maintain a level of professional courtesy with the professor. If you are the type of person who holds grudges due to past slights and perceived injustices, this may not be the role for you. More importantly, if the whole instruction staff feels the same way, no one else will want to teach for the professor in question, and you'll be asked to cover classes no one else wants. One instruction coordinator spoke of how frustrating it was to have to ask other librarians who were already overburdened to teach more classes. There was a point in the semester where the coordinators could see that the librarians they supervised were getting near their breaking points in terms of too many classes to teach. One coordinator felt that he had to take on these classes himself because he knew that the rest of his instructors did not have the energy. This is a fairly common experience of many librarians, and there is no perfect solution. If people are overbooked, then perhaps it is time to start turning down class requests, but to turn down class requests is to risk never getting those requests again. A wise library coordinator will turn down a request in a way that makes it clear that it is an issue of time and capacity, offering ways professors can get similar services that semester and asking them to schedule earlier in the semester next time.

Scheduling Takes Up Time

With very few exceptions, when discussing parts of the job that they did *not* like, most coordinators focused on how hard it was to manage the logistics of which classes were taught in what locations. In many cases, people noted that they loved the people they worked with and loved being in a classroom but felt utterly unprepared for the pragmatic details of a job that often dealt very little with teaching and much more with management. They were also trying to find ways to make sure that multiple classes were taught on time and in a place that could accommodate the needs of that specific class. Many felt that they could handle the interpersonal issues of working with others on a day-to-day basis, and interactions with other information literacy librarians were rarely the sources of conflict; rather, it was when they were working with teaching faculty that challenges arose. Sometimes these struggles stemmed from not having many spaces within the library to work with and then having to be aware of what other spaces were available on campus. Some professors want to hold their classes at the same time, but even if you have the manpower to deal with these requests, there is simply the practical need to find a space for these classes. Librarians who dealt with larger campuses and commuter campuses talked about these struggles the most, but even those on smaller campuses (smaller student populations or just smaller physical spaces) noted these issues. From a practical standpoint, many coordinators discussed that trying to schedule everyone and make sure that everyone was in the same loop often took up a majority of their time so that they had less time to focus on other areas of their work during that busy season.

One common point of conflict with scheduling is that even after a room has been scheduled, higher-priority issues will arise, which means last-minute rescheduling and shifting of spaces. Sometimes a higher authority will want to use the space, or the class you were sure when you scheduled it only had eight students in it actually has fifty students and needs to be held in a different space. You may try to smooth out and prevent many of these hiccups beforehand, but some small issues simply cannot be forethought. Although it might seem easier to have multiple instruction spaces to help with scheduling burdens, it can often create more madness, as classes and content professors get confused about which location they are supposed to be at, or sometimes regular semester-long classes become scheduled in one of your rooms, and now the room cannot be booked for library instruction during that time multiple times a week. You will be lucky if these issues do not happen during a busy instruction time. Of instruction coordinators who had to factor in scheduling rooms that had regular semester-long classes in them, they found that they had to keep multiple factors in mind, including basic functionality, such as making sure people outside the library had keys to the rooms. One coordinator wrote that typically librarians would have keys to the instruction rooms, but when outside content professors needed access to the space, they had to either have another key cut for this person and make sure that it was returned at the end of the semester or, in one case, make sure that someone was around to lock and unlock the room for professors. Even making sure that a room has the right supplies for a specific class held that day can take up a lot of time. For example, if an instruction coordinator knows that one class will be using laptops, he or she will need to make sure they are charged in time for the class, have no accessibility problems, and are available in the room. Sometimes the space may be available but the laptops have already been reserved by another class or librarian for other purposes. Other items, such as projectors or AV equipment, may need to be set up ahead of time.

A few applications and resources can help ease the burden of scheduling. These calendars and time managers can be good independently but often help most when there is buy-in from the group at large. The most popular application at the moment is Google Calendar, because it is free and syncs seamlessly with many other applications librarians may already be using. Slowly making inroads, though, are products from Springshare, such as LibCal and LibStaffer, that can help schedule and book librarians in public-facing tools. Unlike Google Calendar, these are paid services, and pricing varies per institution. In the earlier chapters on technology, this was addressed in more detail.

As Kim Pittman, a coordinator at a state college, put it, "Many people within my library are most aware of the logistical component of my job, like scheduling library sessions...I'm always trying to minimize the amount of time I spend on those tasks in order to focus more on pedagogy, assessment, etc." Frequently, these logistical tasks are easy to see from an outsider's perspective, yet because they are so visible, it can be hard to show off the more time-consuming portions of the job. Highlighting and emphasizing the invisible portions of the job to others can be conflicting. Many instructors wrote that they had to purposely schedule time in their own calendars so that they could work on their own independent projects or even just catch up on literature in the field. It is easy to get overwhelmed by and wrapped up in the logistical, day-to-day areas of the work and forget other aspects of the job. Librarians in smaller institutions spoke about this, frequently citing the fact that they needed to wear many hats and often had to leave one area of their roles underserved in order to maintain the coordinator role. When retirements increase, along with the budget decreases that many libraries have already seen, it is not uncommon for librarians and instruction coordinators to find themselves in charge of many services that are not part of their original job descriptions, often without an increase in pay or added benefits. Aside from the fact that this can add to stress and weaken services, it is important for instruction coordinators to speak with their supervisors or deans and ask how much of their time should be spend on each task. When you have a better sense of how much time is needed for each area, you can better schedule your own workflow. Scheduling can mean managing classroom instruction, but it can also mean managing your other roles. For those librarians who choose to schedule their own learning time, it can often be just an hour or two blocked off as research time with a specific theme. The hardest part is honoring that time without letting other projects or meetings slip into that dedicated time. In writing about why she chose to honor this blocked-off time in her schedule, Pittman wrote, "Balancing this kind of work with my teaching load is an ongoing process," with a reiteration that these were priorities for her, and if she did not get time to focus on them, they would never be accomplished.

From a very practical perspective, making others aware of the instruction schedule is one often overlooked detail that can save others from confusion or mistakes. Although there are fancy ways to go about it, all that really needs to happen is for the schedule for each classroom to be posted at the beginning of each day. This alerts others of who will be in the room and at what times,

Determining Workflow

List your typical duties in the first column. In the next column, list how much time you need for each activity per week. Then look at your actual schedule and see how much time is really being devoted to each task.

Instruction Prep → 2 hrs. per class → 0 hrs. per class
Reference → 6 hrs. → 4 hrs./week
Collection Development → 6 hrs. → 8 hrs./week
University Committee Work → 2 hrs./committee → 3 hrs./committee

Using this chart, you can gain a sense of where your time is currently going and look for realistic ways to restructure that time. Use it as a starting point for a conversation with your supervisor.

which is handy for librarians, of course, but also helps students who may use these classrooms as study spaces or open computer labs when the space is not in use. In my own personal experience, we brought about this strategy because although all the librarians were aware of the schedule from our shared online calendar, increasingly students within the classroom space were engaged in intensive projects that could not easily be set aside. This tended to happen during afternoon and evening classes, when students assumed that the space would be open because most classes were done for the day. Sometimes students were more than happy to move to other computers elsewhere in the library, but frequently they were in the middle of intensive projects (or once in the middle of an online exam that couldn't be retaken). In situations like these, you are more likely than not to leave bad tastes in the mouths of both students and instructors. Finding ways to avoid negative experiences is vital for an instruction coordinator.

There are fancy electronic digital signage systems from companies like Creston, Steelcase, and Quartet, among others, but if your library does not have the funds to invest in digital signage at the moment, there are old-fashioned options, such as whiteboards and paper. Even creating a simplified digital sign by using an old monitor and running a few simple PowerPoint slides can help effectively communicate the schedule. By posting a paper schedule on the doors or door frames of each classroom, we were able to cut down on the chances of having to kick students out of the classroom. If you are concerned about personal details being visible to all who pass by, try not to add personally identifiable information, such as the instructor name—just the course details. Or if those details are necessary for the online calendar, they can be temporarily edited out when printing and then added back in. Another common frustration point for putting up the calendar is just the act of remembering to do it when classes are in session, particularly as this tends to be our busiest time of the year. In this case, instruction coordinators can put up the schedule for the whole week instead. Oftentimes when we try to think of solutions that make it easier for us, we focus on ourselves, but working in a complex academic ecosystem like a university means that you'll have to consider the needs of your most valuable users, the students.

> The difference between leading the team and simply being a part of the team is a striking contrast. When leading, brainstorming ideas aloud can have different weight than when you are "just" a team member. —Donna Witek, University of Scranton

Listening and Speaking Up

Many coordinators spent a lot of time listening to their instruction librarians to get a greater sense of how the team felt about decisions, content professors, and day-to-day departmental decisions. Sometimes this was in regard to larger pedagogy, and other times it was day to day concerns. Some coordinators felt as though they often held the swing vote for big departmental decisions, but tried to reflect the needs of their department. Others found that it was easier to make decisions with their teams if they all dedicated time to communicating their needs. Many instruction coordinators held weekly or biweekly meetings with everyone on the team in order to get a sense of what was happening in instruction and see if there were any ongoing issues they could help fix or move along in any way. There is no perfect style, and there are certainly gendered issues associated with asking people to listen.[2] In some senses, it will be on you to figure out where to draw the line, but just being aware of the gendered issues involved with this work can help.

Differences in Institutions

When I began my research on the topic of instruction coordinators, I assumed that there would be major differences between the type of institution and how coordination was performed. In reality, coordination may differ more due to organizational culture than institution size. A host of reasons influence how a program is run, such as personality and cultural and educational background. Indeed, many differences stemmed from a lack of funding or a lack of support from the institution rather than differences in structure. The largest structural differences came from institutions that had the creative ability to experiment more than others, either through a large support system of many instruction librarians or through a particularly engaged staff.

Within the classroom, instruction did not vary much from institution to institution. There were natural differences in how instruction was performed, but these differences tended to align more closely with instructor preference rather than a driven pedagogical approach pushed by an instruction program. At most, these differences were focused on the types of resources available, such as more-expensive databases or a lack of adequate computers. That said, the detailed differences between institutions were on the logistical side, such as how scheduling was managed and who took on the bulk of it. In many larger institutions, the instruction coordinator only scheduled freshman-level 101 courses, and subject liaisons were responsible for their own class scheduling. Most coordinators felt that this relieved a large burden of the scheduling responsibility, but then it gave them the added responsibility of trying to keep track of what classes were being taught for their own statistical and assessment uses. There are natural differences in style and the current information literacy program's focus. For example, a few programs lean away from one-shots and toward a longer-term information literacy model.

In addition, although everyone agreed that they were busy, the capacity level of instruction filled up varying on size. Many libraries were understaffed or lacked the ability to teach every English 101 class, or if they could, they were unable to branch out into other areas of instruction, despite their desire to do so. At some point during the curriculum mapping process, instruction coordinators should look at how many instructors they have available to teach and what a realistic maximum capacity is for teaching load. Teaching capacity varies based on institution size and to some degree on the willingness of the teachers themselves, but every institution has a cap for how many classes it can teach per semester. Yes, more manpower will help you increase this capacity, but at a certain point, hiring people just to fill instruction capacity will become unsustainable either because of cost reasons or because of the flux of instruction, and there may be times when you will have extra people on staff who are suddenly left twiddling their thumbs. Many libraries do not have the budgets for this kind of long-term solution either. Instead, look at the curriculum map you created in order to gain a better sense of what areas you want to strategically focus on each semester, and this can give you better grounding for what classes to accept. If the program has reached maximum capacity, it is more than all right to tell a professor that you do not have the space or manpower to teach his or her class that semester. In times like this, it can be handy to have backups to point to, like a well-designed LibGuide or premade worksheets that are frequently used for a specific area. Cara Stone at Grand View University wrote about how curriculum mapping affected her own instruction:

> I truly have an understanding of how what I am doing helps the students not only meet the expectations of the assignment or course, but also how that is intertwined with expectations throughout the curriculum to help them be successful in future courses and beyond in their future employment. The library staff is able to communicate with faculty as they plan curriculum and designate information literacy as an outcome for their course. We have a role in curriculum mapping and course design. We work closely with faculty to develop and scaffold information literacy skills and assignments throughout their course, their departments, and the greater curriculum, and we work with them to implement it in their classes.[3]

Curriculum mapping is not just an exercise in busywork; when applied strategically, it can give meaning and guided structure to a lesson that might otherwise seem unfounded. The unspoken part of this is that as you structure where the lessons are happening this way, they get better and receive better feedback from your professors, because instead of basic demonstrations, professors start getting lessons that fold seamlessly into their own syllabi.

Returning to the idea of how to determine your maximum capacity, there are a few ways to find this number. First, be aware of how many classroom spaces are available to the library. Without a physical location, the request for instruction reaches gridlock very quickly. From there, look at how many class slots are available each day. Usually this is around nine or ten slots, with some variations. Multiplying the number of class slots by classroom spaces gives you a number to deduct from, because—reality check—no one is or should be teaching one-shots nonstop from 8 a.m. to 6 p.m. every day.

State universities and colleges can be research universities, but the ones I focus on here are frequently not the flagship schools of their states but rather the smaller teaching colleges that the state also supports. Their focuses can vary greatly, as can their staff sizes. When talking to one coordinator who had jumped from a large research university to a state teaching college, Elizabeth Galoozis at the University of Southern California said, "I didn't realize what an impact organizational culture makes on a coordinator's work, because I didn't think much about different organizational cultures. I wish I'd taken a little more time to get to know that before going in to coordinator responsibilities." She succinctly narrowed in on a common issue: every organization has their own unique culture that may not react as well to your ideas as others. Naturally, those larger institutions may have a different culture than those smaller ones who rely on other systems. Looking at our organizational culture can take some deeper reflection than we are willing to take on, particularly if it turns out that the mirror reflects something harsher than we wanted to acknowledge. As some instruction coordinators noted in their responses, changing an organizational culture takes a long time, and they often felt that they were not well placed in the institution to instigate that change, believing that this was a change that should be brought about by administration. Indeed, usually this is so, but some instruction coordinators spoke at length about how they dealt with differing attitudes within themselves and how they interacted with others.

One focus in particular was on the topic of LibGuides. Since their arrival within the library world in 2007, they have spread rapidly due to their flexibility and usability. In addition, paper handout use has decreased since the arrival of LibGuides, which is a good point to bear in mind for those learners who need a physical copy to refer back to, and some students may not be thriving with the use of LibGuides. In particular, many instruction coordinators are using these guides as a place to store library evaluation links and lesson plans and as a location for their instruction coordinators to drop in and gather resources during class prep. Although all types of institutions use LibGuides at this point, the primary group was smaller institutions that are responsible for the majority of their own web maintenance and development. This could be an issue of budget and ability to leverage one type of resource for many others. Particularly with library evaluations, many instruction programs are housing the links to their student and faculty evaluations with a combined use of LibGuides and Google Forms. Another added benefit to housing these links at these locations is that most student and faculty users at this point will be used to these interfaces and will not be hesitant to submit evaluations. Libraries are moving away from using paper-based forms for evaluation, and it falls upon the instruction coordinator to find ways to disseminate the information submitted over these systems.

The Best Coordinators Have a Strong Support System

It became very clear to me that while coordinators could find ways to survive and thrive in a nonsupportive environment, the ones who truly flourished had support systems from within the institution, through either supervisors who wanted to offer advice or organizations that were receptive to their ideas. Many coordinators spoke about shadowing people on the job before they took over the role or of deans who gave them the support to go to conferences and learn how to establish a program. Usually these people were those who had filled the role before them. In one case, someone went to another local institution that already had a flourishing instruction program to gather details on what was needed. Of those who felt unsupported, it was often not because of overt antagonism but rather a lack of interest in instruction from those above them. Some coordinators felt that they were fighting uphill battles when they had to lobby for new things such as training and classroom time. One coordinator wrote that although she was given verbal support, the expectations that came with the role were so outsized that she felt as though the words were meaningless. It can sometimes be very hard to differentiate between a person who is outwardly nice and one who is supportive, especially during the interview process, when you may be completely new to the organization and trying to parse the differences between what is said and what is actually meant. The supervisors who showed support for coordinators were frequently the ones who checked in on progress and not only offered words of encouragement but also understood what was needed from instruction and sought out inventive ways to encourage the instruction department. One coordinator said that the best way she was able to get other departments to take advantage of library instruction was through encouragement from her supervisor, who allowed her to participate in outside committees that were not directly related to her work but gave her networking opportunities that showed outside faculty members the value of information literacy and instruction. Another common train of thought was that the coordinators were lucky to have the frameworks and systems that had been set up before them, because they often felt that when they arrived in their new roles, they had little understanding of just what the position involved and felt that without the prior frameworks, they would have been lost. This is not to imply that we need to firmly uphold the precedents laid down for us by our predecessors; there should always be a degree of flexibility and uniqueness within a role so that we can be comfortable. However, knowing the background of a role can give us the grounding for how we want to change it and steer the course for the future. One instruction coordinator was promoted into the role from within the institution. The prior coordinator was still working in the institution, so she initially felt hampered by the need to make sure that no changes felt like a slap to the face of the prior coordinator. Those coordinators who came into the role after the prior coordinator had left (or the role was nonexistent before) had a much different experience.

Understandably, while coordinators who had strong support systems were eager to share about their experiences with good leaders, those who had bad or even neutral responses were hesitant to give feedback on what it was like to try to establish programs without strong support. Those who gave information often did not want to be named. In some ways, this can be one of the limiters to the profession. The best things shine and are brought up within the community, but despite the profession's growth, we are still a very small and insular profession. The connections and associations we make with one another can have ripple effects farther along in our careers. With that caveat, problems with a lack of support are discussed here with a trusting attitude. Those who felt unsupported as they took on their roles felt that they had to essentially create their jobs and job descriptions. Though they may have been given loose guidelines, many felt that when they came into the role, they were blind about the practical details and had to figure them out through a trial-and-error process.

Summary

Instruction coordinators range in age and library type, with many coordinators using unique methods to accommodate their institutional practices. No one style works for every situation, but many libraries have found that continuing to learn and working on finding ways to work with others on management issues, particularly scheduling, can pay off in the long run.

NOTES

1. Ann E. Austin, "Preparing the Next Generation of Faculty: Graduate School as Socialization to the Academic Career," *Journal of Higher Education* 73, no. 1 (2002): 94–122.
2. Veronica Arellano Douglas and Joanna Gadsby, "Gendered Labor and Library Instruction Coordinators," ACRL conference paper, March 2017, 266–74.
3. Cara B. Stone in survey from author, January 3, 2017.

FURTHER READINGS

Austin, Ann E. "Preparing the Next Generation of Faculty: Graduate School as Socialization to the Academic Career." *Journal of Higher Education* 73, no. 1 (2002): 94–122.

Douglas, Veronica Arellano, and Joanna Gadsby. "Gendered Labor and Library Instruction Coordinators." ACRL conference paper, March 2017.

Afterword

When you look through job ads for instruction coordinators, a few common themes arise in the descriptions and preferred qualifications. Often phrases like "proven leadership" and "experience with the framework" pop up. For librarians who are thinking of applying for these positions, particularly newer librarians, it may seem as though it is impossible to get these positions because they lack "demonstrated skills" in these particular areas. The language of job advertisements focuses on finding the perfect person, sometimes one who may not even exist in the real world, but what separates those who end up being hired from those who were not is often less a difference in their resumes or vitae and much more a difference in interviewing skills. Hiring employees is one of the riskier tasks a company can take on, because an unknown factor is being added into the community, and certainly HR takes care to minimize those costs and risks with carefully worded job descriptions. Throughout this book, I have discussed what makes instruction coordinators unique and what it takes to thrive within the role. Many of these skills do not come instinctively but rather take time to grow and be nourished by mentors and other leaders. The path toward becoming an effective instruction coordinator is a learning curve that is not always clear-cut, and likely the situations that test you will come faster and sooner than you would like.

I outlined the different types of instruction coordinators in chapter 1, particularly how they got their roles and what specific challenges they faced. Introspection was prominent in these responses as people reflected on what they loved and what they wished they could have done over again. Looking at their specific words and actions, we can see a common pathway. Although each has different attitudes, techniques, and reactions, it all came from a place of trying to promote information literacy and a love of instruction. When we focus on what brought us to librarianship, it is easier to remember the nicer parts of our jobs, find meaning, and focus on our individual tasks.

Next Steps

Having read this book, one of the actions you can now take as either an incumbent instruction coordinator or an instruction coordinator currently working in the field is to note what your current practice looks like. It may be that you find the current workflow to be perfectly satisfactory—in which case, congratulations! If certain sections of this book piqued your interest or made you wonder how an idea would play out in your situation, I encourage you to at minimum look at ways that you could explore or modify it for your library. This job has no uniform, and that gives us the liberty to try on as many different roles as we would like. The scale of the job of an instruction coordinator at one institution can be vastly different from that of an institution across the country. Finding and making time to read library literature can be hard when we keep busy schedules that include committee work and our own tenure and promotion activities. Look through the list of resources in each chapter, try to find at least one article or book that interests you, and block out time to read into the field. Also, remind yourself that you are not alone in this field. There are lots of instruction coordinators, and we can learn from each other, even if it is to serve as a sounding board for mistakes and frustrations. Reach out to regional contacts and see if there are avenues that would lead to natural collaboration.

Reaching Out: Creating a Network of Like-Minded Coordinators

- Participate on ALA Connect. The ACRL Instruction Section has a lively discussion forum. Identify coordinators in your region.
- Ask to observe at another institution.
- Consider hosting a local coordinator "unconference" or retreat.
  Sometimes people think of these things as being a lot of work, but they can be as simple as a space to meet, a set of questions sent ahead of time, and a pot of coffee.
  If it works well, repeat once a year or even semester!
- Attend local conferences and speak out.
  Conferences are only as strong as the material proposed.
  Start volunteering on committees related to instruction.

You won't feel comfortable doing everything yourself, and you should not feel the need to do it all, but even finding one information literacy buddy or ally who puts thought into the profession can encourage you to think differently or give you options on how to approach a problem that might be giving you pause. Connections can strengthen our work and encourage us to try new things without a fear of failing. They can also illustrate what we do not want in our programs. The "one small thing" approach of attempting at least a portion of a new thing can get you set up on the road toward making new connections and finding your strengths with new lesson plans and management techniques.

Follow-Up

Sometimes the instruction coordinator role can be seen as a step up to greater leadership roles. For others, this is the primary goal. They love instruction, and they are content to spend their work life focusing on it. However, we can attend the best conferences, read the right literature, and speak to the top people in the field, but if we are not finding ways to meaningfully employ and take action on the things we study and learn about we are wasting our time. One of the easiest ways you can take advantage of the ideas found in this book is to set up meetings with your chair or dean and get a sense of where they want the department to go as a whole, if you do not already have this information at hand. Having a conceptual frame for how to bring about change at the forefront of library instruction can give clarity to where decisions are made and for what purpose. Likewise, make time to listen to what your instructors want. Are they really interested in trying out new techniques and tips, or are they happy with their current information literacy process? Having that conversation will give you a greater sense of what is feasible with your team and how far you can stretch them.

Make a goal for each week, each month, and each semester for who you want to get to know and specifically what information you can give them and they can give you. Sometimes it will take repeated attempts to get people to respond or listen to you, but more frequently, most people are enthusiastic and willing to have a cup of coffee and listen to you. Some people will write brief ideas that they want to go over on note cards, and others will just have one core issue that they use to cover their bases.

Finally, with the exception of a few rigidly bound roles, the role of instruction coordinator can be incredibly flexible and modified to your skillset. Figuring out how you lead best will not be an overnight process, but with time and through observing case studies and staying attuned to the literature of the field, you will eventually find the way to be an instruction coordinator that works for your unique situation, specific to you and your patrons.

My hope is that this book has given you and your instruction department ideas to ponder but more importantly try out. There may be things here that will not work for your situation, but starting the process of thinking critically about the roles of the instruction coordinator is always a great step forward.

Survey Questions

1. What is your title?

2. What got you involved with instruction?

3. What surprised you most about being a coordinator?

4. What part of your job do you wish others knew or understood better?

5. What is your favorite / least favorite part of your role in instruction?

6. If you could go back to library school knowing you would be heavily involved in instruction management, what classes would you take?

7. Do you feel instruction differs at a [x institution] compared to other types of institutions? If so, how?

8. Reflecting on your time as a coordinator, what mistakes come to mind? What would you do to avoid them?

9. What is your attitude toward managing and scheduling other instruction librarians? Do you have direct supervision over anyone?

10. What's your number-one tip for other instruction coordinators or librarians thinking about taking on the job?

11. What kind of support as an instruction coordinator did you receive from your institution when you were new to the role?

Index